Who's the Entrepreneur?

The BizFizz Story: unleashing the passion, transforming communities

A business coaching-networking approach to regeneration

Helping people to pursue their passion is the first step for BizFizz. Removing the barriers that stand in their way is what BizFizz is all about.

Is there anyone out there who wants to do something?

The stories contained in this book are an invitation to activists, entrepreneurs, professionals and students of regeneration, business support and development to challenge the very basis of support systems and development project approaches both in the UK and internationally. To all of the people who have the appetite to challenge the status quo, and the curiosity to seek alternative visions of the future - we invite you to join the value-driven approach to change – one versed in the belief in individuals and the combined power of their dreams to transform their communities.

Who's the Entrepreneur?

The *BizFizz* Story: unleashing the passion, transforming communities

A business coaching-networking approach to regeneration

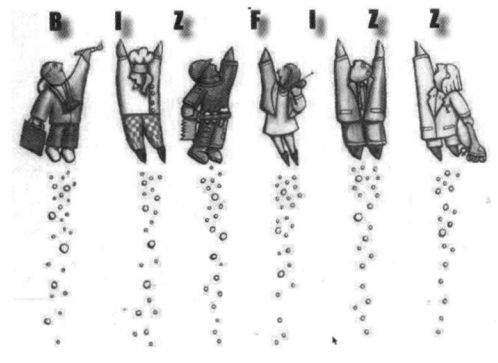

Edited by Paul Squires, Elizabeth Cox and David Boyle

nef (the new economics foundation)
Civic Trust

Acknowledgements

This book reflects the experience of the BizFizz programme, a joint
venture between the Civic Trust and **nef**, and draws out the lessons to
effectively support entrepreneurs from within their own communities,
particularly in those experiencing economic disadvantage. We high-
light the powerful role that enterprise, when supported by the wider
community, can play to regenerate a community. The book is largely
written by practicing BizFizz coaches who have lived and breathed the
role for the past two years. It also reflects the experience of everyone
involved in the programme and is a tribute to their enormous effort
and imagination – particularly the two people who did most to launch
it: Bernie Ward and Mikyla Robinson.

Special thanks is also extended to Alison Ball, Fred Forshaw, Elliot
Patterson and Keith Jeffrey, challenging professionals whose coaching
experiences piloting the model were invaluable to its development.

This book is dedicated to all those entrepreneurs and communities
who came on the journey with us. We hope this book will help
unleash similar passion and success in other communities both in
the UK and further afield.

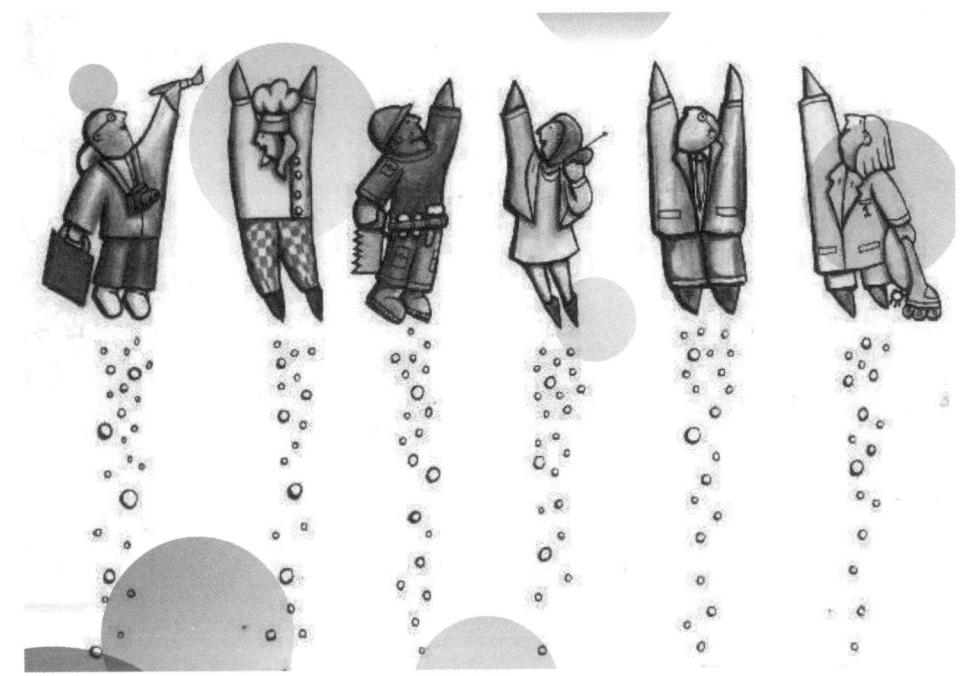

WHO'S THE ENTREPRENEUR?

The BizFizz Story: unleashing the passion, transforming communities

nef is an independent think-and-do tank that inspires and demonstrates real economic well-being.

We aim to improve quality of life by promoting innovative solutions that challenge mainstream thinking on economic, environmental and social issues. We work in partnership and put people and the planet first.

The Civic Trust is an urban environment charity concerned with improving the quality of life in our towns, cities and villages.

economics
real wealth
means well-being

Current priorities include international debt, transforming markets, global finance and local economic renewal

environment
lifestyles must
become sustainable

Current priorities are climate change, ecological debt and local sustainability

society
communities need
power and influence

Current priorities include democracy, time banks, well-being and public services

nef (new economics foundation) is a registered charity founded in 1986 by the leaders of The Other Economic Summit (TOES), which forced issues such as international debt onto the agenda of the G7/G8 summit meetings. It has taken a lead in helping establish new coalitions and organisations, such as the Jubilee 2000 debt campaign; the Ethical Trading Initiative; the UK Social Investment Forum; and new ways to measure social and environmental well-being.

Contents

List of contributors

David Boyle is an associate at **nef**, and in that capacity has helped launch organisations like Time Banks UK, has written widely about the future of money and volunteering and has edited reports on co-production and the future of the NHS. He is the author of books including *The Tyranny of Numbers* and *Authenticity.*

Elizabeth Cox is head of the Connected Economies Programme at **nef,** an economist by training, she has moved from lecturing on development and agricultural economics in Aberdeen University to policy work within the Ministry of Agriculture in Guyana. These experiences led to **nef** and BizFizz, where as project manager, she was responsible – with colleagues at the Civic Trust – for piloting and developing the BizFizz programme. Her work at **nef** continues to challenge top-down approaches to regeneration, and systems which smother action and passion in communities in the UK and internationally.

Paul Davies is the BizFizz coach for Clowne in north east Derbyshire. Previously he had been running a consultancy business, working mainly for large companies and public sector organisations. In 2005, Paul was awarded the Institute of Business Advisers' 'Adviser of the Year' award for his work with BizFizz. He lives in Chesterfield with his wife and two children.

Vicky Evans is the BizFizz coach in the town of Winsford in Cheshire. She also works as a learning coach in a high school in North Wales . Her coaching business, Passion for Life, specialises in supporting people to find and live their passions.

Natalia Fernandez was the BizFizz coach for Leicester. Her background prior to running her own business in corporate coaching and coaching gifted children in inner city schools was as a business development manager in higher and further education. This work also provided the opportunity to travel and generate new income streams. BizFizz gave her the opportunity to work directly with the community.

Anne Francis is a BizFizz business coach and has been involved in regeneration work for many years. She was instrumental in setting up the first credit union and fair trade outlet in Norwich and a regional network for businesswomen. She has also been involved in establish-

3

ing micro-finance in Norfolk and is passionate about bringing people together from diverse backgrounds.

Lynne Jones is the national co-ordinator for BizFizz, working with the Civic Trust. Lynne joined BizFizz from Barnados, and brings over 25 years of strategic and operational management experience to the team. Her background is in retail and management development and she understands the highs and lows of being self-employed having opened a family run shop in 2003.

Stefan Nichols is a co-active coach with many years' experience at the coal face of community development. An entrepreneur by nature, with a passion for creating safe spaces where people can explore their full potential, Stefan is currently developing his leadership skills and challenging his own boundaries, including writing a book about coaching techniques.

Mark Shipperlee left school at 17 because he wanted to work outdoors, and was frustrated by school. By 22, he had his own tree-surgery business in south east England and went on to set up an international charity in response to a visit to Romania immediately after the collapse of the Iron Curtain, which grew to a £2-million turnover. After ten years at the helm, he stepped aside to take on international project development work for Big Issue Scotland. Mark is currently the BizFizz coach in the Alnwick area and is also a director of the not-for-profit company Local Living.

Paul Squires is a regeneration consultant at the Civic Trust who develops programmes of work that place enterprise at the heart of regeneration and regenerating communities. His involvement with BizFizz started in 2001 and is currently the project manager of the BizFizz programme for the Civic Trust.

Peter Waistell is our first 'serial' BizFizz coach, having first BizFizzed in the Stanley Green Corridor and then moving across to Weardale. Before that, he was surviving in the East Midlands as a corporate manager for a major bank. He prefers working to help businesses enhance a community, rather than enhancing PLC profits. He supports Hartlepool United and deals with his frustrations by playing golf (for which he receives regular coaching).

Prologue
A second look at Toxteth

Stefan Nichols

"Money is a by-product of entrepreneurial success, and very welcome it is, but it isn't the heart of it. Entrepreneurs change the world first, even in very small ways. They see something new that others don't. They imagine the world differently."
Anita Roddick

"BizFizz gives you what you need when the other advisors just give you the same information they give everyone who comes through their door. For the others it's just a job they are paid to do – and at the end of the meeting, they reach into their drawer and pull out a load of forms that they have to give you."
BizFizz client in Toxteth

Two stories

The judge was summing up. From where we sat, sideways on to the proceeding, things looked hopeless. You could actually hear the distinct sound made by the closing of the prison door. The rattle of keys followed by metallic clank as the door closed, which was followed by the final jangling of the warden's keys, the sliding of the viewing flap back and forth… and then silence. The opening sequence of *Porridge* with Ronnie Barker sprang to mind. The awful reality of a waste of this precious life, of unfulfilled potential, of what could have been possible, began to sink in.

"I have reviewed the submissions from the various contributors", said the Judge in a softly spoken but unmistakably authoritative voice, "and in passing sentence I should let you know now that because of your BizFizz coach and the strong supportive statement he submitted, you will not be going to prison." The audible gasp from the client's supporters and friends sitting around me will remain an endearing memory. The client walked free with an order to seek support from a local mentoring service. BizFizz has continued to support this client and over the past months he has gone on to build his business and to date employs eight local people. His community, seen as isolated and insular, has begun to place some trust in BizFizz.

A three-page business plan fit only for the bin was all the client had to show from 18 months of mentoring and support from a national business support agency. He was distraught, his dreams in tatters, his life wrecked. "I thought of ending it all, I was so low", he said at our first meeting. He was angry, raging actually, his emotions pouring out of him in a torrent. That day we began the journey of what was possible. During the journey the client hit the bottom again and again, and each time he got up for more. Slowly we developed the plan. We found some great people working in agencies and pooled our skills and support. If this client could make it, just get into business, then anything was possible, anyone else seeing this happen would know that they could make it, too.

Long-term unemployed, on disability allowance, black, bad credit rating, no assets, surviving from hand to mouth with not enough money to even get to the next meeting, written off by people as a dreamer and a no-hoper the client inched forward, stuck to his values and principles, accepted the hard road, and refused to turn back when even I thought we were drowning. He had drive, passion, energy, determination, anger, values, and principles and he used them all to reach out for the dream of starting his own business and creating a different future for himself.

On 22 March 2006, with the support of some courageous people – many of whom had gone out on a professional limb – the client ordered his executive travel vehicle from the United States of America. His dream had come true; his future had become another journey. A short film is now being made of this man's struggle to own his own dream. George Cover is a local hero and an inspiration to all. He embodies the Toxteth entrepreneurial spirit.

The Toxteth Story

A quarter of a century ago this year, Toxteth acquired for itself an unenviable reputation for urban hopelessness and violence. The first weekend in July – just three weeks before Prince Charles's wedding, and following the Brixton and Southall riots – Toxteth witnessed scenes that have, in the words of the local MP, "never been witnessed in a British city under the rule of law this century". At the height of the destruction, when rioters burned buildings to within 200 yards of the Anglican cathedral, geriatric patients had to be evacuated from their homes by taxi. Looters – some of them as young as five years old – queued to get into the shops, and police lines faced a bizarre attack by a stolen fleet of Unigate milkfloats. It marked the first time that CS gas had been used in a mainland city in Britain.

"Walking around the streets of Liverpool afterwards, I saw what living in the inner city really means," said the then Environment Secretary Michael Heseltine, minister responsible for cities. "But amid the personal tragedy and public disorder, something good emerged, because we were forced to rethink our strategy for the inner cities."

Having appointed himself Minister for Merseyside, Heseltine described conditions there on television in shocked tones. "Dreadful, dreadful," he said. What emerged out of this and subsequent visits was the Merseyside Task Force, the Merseyside Development Agency, the Liverpool Garden Festival, and a whole alphabet of acronyms and grant mechanisms that have made up the background to the lives of those trying to improve run-down neighbourhoods over the past quarter century. In short, Toxteth's travails – by far the worst of the 1981 riots – gave birth to an industry in its own right: Liverpool's regeneration industry.

A great deal has changed since that time. The original causes of the blight that lay behind so many of the 1981 riots – most of the riot zones were designated for inner urban motorway schemes that were never built – have been removed. There is a greater understanding and intolerance towards racism. Regeneration is a profession where practitioners can become national figures on large salaries, and spend their entire careers in the sector. So we have to ask – and this is the question that lies behind this book – why, even after all of the regeneration money that has poured into Liverpool and other similar areas, has so little of the fabric of these places actually changed? Why do they continue to be awarded the Government classification of deprived areas?

King James' ancient hunting park, known as Toxteth, has certainly been through its share of hard times. It is immediately south of Liverpool city centre, and has fantastic views over the River Mersey and the Welsh hills, but it remains a synonym for urban decay and unrest. Toxteth has received just about all of the regeneration funding initiatives that successive governments have announced over the last 20 years, yet there is still little difference in how the area looks.

One key characteristic of this community is its fragmentation. Toxteth's black community is one of the oldest in the country. More recently a Somali population and a Yemeni community have moved into the area. These remain distinct and rarely meet, with people from one street never mixing with people from another. There is also suspicion in Toxteth of outside regeneration agencies that 'move in and then back out' with short-term programmes that make little difference, at least none that lasts.

There are some roads with new housing association homes, but there are also several streets where the majority of the housing is boarded up. The physical decline is matched with social statistics – the area has one of the highest rates of child poverty in the country. Toxteth has by far the highest unemployment rate in Liverpool City at 13.3 per cent. Liverpool was ranked first in the 1998 *Index of Local Deprivation* and the Toxteth wards within the area are some of the most deprived in the city.

But when you put aside statistics for a moment, which neither describe the people nor the place very accurately, and look at what is really there, then the paradox of British urban regeneration becomes very clear. There is another side to Toxteth, which is very different. Indeed, it has probably always been so.

If you read the statistics, you might be forgiven for believing that the flyblown buildings and peeling paint are somehow a reflection of the people who live there. You might imagine that successful regeneration is somehow a matter of outsiders parachuting in and setting up business or simply paying the bills. In fact, one of the most valuable but little-understood resources in Toxteth – and in similar neighbourhoods all over Britain – is its people; to be more precise, its entrepreneurs. There may be a shortage of money, at least below agency level, but there are plenty of entrepreneurs in Toxteth, some of them operating in the informal economy, but many people just wanting to earn a living from doing something they enjoy.

Take Toxteth TV for example, set up by a group of dynamic entrepreneurs to provide a creative hub right in the middle of the area on Windsor Street. It is a striking building with coloured, striped brickwork and built with low cost materials on the site of a shut pub.
There is workspace for small businesses, studio and production facilities, courses and meeting space. It is a hotbed of new talent and creative energy. Four of the founding entrepreneurs invited a BizFizz coach to operate out of the Toxteth TV building, so it is also central to the story that this book seeks to tell.

This book tells the story of another way forward for regeneration, and the peculiar tale of the hidden entrepreneurs that are beginning to make an enormous difference to the places where they live – including Toxteth. It is about this hidden resource, these innovative people operating below the radar of government statistics, often attracting deep official suspicion, and what they mean for regeneration. They are people who see the world a little differently and are prepared to put that vision into practice. They are as much a headache for official regenerators as they are a resource. While one official agency is trying to prevent them claiming benefit or receiving any other kind of business support, another official agency is trying to force their business ideas into shapes that fit the agency's particular targets.

The BizFizz Story
This is the story of a business coaching idea called BizFizz, the people behind it, and how they set about finding a way to provide genuine support to those who can really transform their communities through enterprise, and turn the rules of regeneration on their head.

It is a story of an approach that eschews marketing of all kinds and deliberately avoids all forms of promotion except word-of-mouth. It is an approach that puts relationships at the heart of what drives them and refuses to be bound by government targets. Believing that the key to business success is who you know rather than simply what you know, it builds teams of support around entrepreneurs. It is an approach that looks at the supposedly hopeless corners of Britain – those which have provided secure incomes for a generation of regeneration officials but remain the development deserts they originally were – and sees and mobilises the hidden assets that economists and policy-makers so rarely recognise. It is an approach that is about very little things – the equivalent of a butterfly's wings flapping over China that are famously supposed to change the weather over here – that make an enormous difference.

To understand this story, you have to see Toxteth differently: not through the distorting prism of its reputation, or of the network of inter-connected official institutions and agencies, pouring money into the area but so crippled by targets that they are often useless, competitive and occasionally deeply destructive, but underneath where you will find a hotbed of talent and creativity where passions focused on business are being unleashed.

The BizFizz story is about what can happen when official targets and jaded institutional bias are put aside; when support agencies, instead take a coaching approach that focuses support on the individual client, build up the necessary trust and credibility to enable people to follow their passion. By unleashing this passion and the resourcefulness, creativity and entrepreneurial flair of the people who live in these places we see a flow of self-confidence and a solution-focused approach to life that is at the very heart of transforming these communities.

Please don't misunderstand. The agencies are necessary, and so are the resources they can access. The problem so often is that they are hidebound by the way they are controlled. We are not advocating the kind of freewheeling buccaneering concept of enterprise where, if only the government gets off the backs of the people, then everything will come right; there are structural problems in places like Toxteth that have prevented that for generations. Nor are we advocating the kind of bogus entrepreneurialism where the wealthy and powerful simply move in and push out everyone else. We are saying that places like Toxteth have vital resources that have become the object of suspicion in the mainstream regeneration industry – the people of Toxteth.

The BizFizz story is also about the development of a whole new kind of regeneration professional – a business coach who has no targets or boxes to tick; who is completely client focused; who is absolutely independent of strings or official agenda; and who does whatever it takes to support local people to achieve their dreams.

So let's take a look at Toxteth though the lens of my experience as a BizFizz coach there. After nearly two years, and without advertising or marketing my services – in other words solely by recommendation – I have been approached by more than 100 potential entrepreneurs looking for support. This number is rising daily. People only come back if they want to and if their experience is a positive one.

This model of regeneration is mysteriously different from the official one. It includes a coaching relationship between two equals focused on meeting the needs of the client. It accepts that the client is naturally resourceful, creative and whole, borrowing as much from the expertise of counselling as it does from business schools. It addresses the client's whole life. The client makes the agenda, which starts from where they are.

As well as the coaches and clients, there is a volunteer panel of local experts drawn from all sectors – people with their own expertise and networks, people who want to help others succeed. Through this panel, coaches can open up a world of positive options, market intelligence, and temporary teams who can support local entrepreneurs through the various stages of development. Through this unusual alliance – coach, client and local panel –problems can be solved, contacts can be made and more opportunities can be opened up.

The coach does not motivate, initiate or chase up clients. Clients take responsibility for their own decisions. With no targets or outputs to deliver, the coach can concentrate on the client, helping them to develop useful networks. The coach does not have to cling to clients to meet targets – clients can be referred to other agencies and still continue the coaching relationship. After a while, clients start to join in the panel or network, and after two years there should be a healthy informal network across the community, which is now experiencing a growing culture of enterprise. What is more, as in Toxteth, clients have started trading with each other so that the work benefits the local area.

The key to working in Toxteth is to build up real trust. One of my first clients was Bangladeshi, and after working with him intensively for five months, he started to introduce me to his friends who are business owners. I started working with a Somali client who has since referred four other clients from the Somali community. A client referring other clients is an important indicator of success for BizFizz. Being based in the community there is nowhere to hide, we have clients because, and only because we are providing good support.

According to Elizabeth Cox, Head of Connected Economies at **nef**, and BizFizz project manager, at the heart of the BizFizz approach there are fundamental values that drive its success and are further expanded upon in the chapters that follow:

- Operating on a trust relationship

- Supporting passionate entrepreneurs

- 100 per cent client-focused support

- Developing support networks

- Mobilising support and resources from within the community

The difficulty is that many of the government agencies dedicated to regeneration regard these hidden resources as extremely unwelcome. In a place like Toxteth, many of the most innovative business ideas start off in the grey economy, and those that start them often want to formalise them – only to be put off by their contact with the official world. There is a genuine fear among people who want to move forward about exposing themselves to officialdom. They are afraid that any probing into their personal circumstances will lead to an even worse financial position, or worse still, accusations may be levelled that impact negatively on their tenuous hold on the economic ladder. Most feel that it is better to stay on their own side of the desert, and remain in their comfort zone. However desperate this may look to outsiders, it is based on hard-learned lessons of economic survival.

Mainstream business advice services are not much better. After a humiliating encounter with an 'expert' where one of my clients was made to feel that business support was intended for successful entrepreneurs, rather than those like her who were single and on the dole, my client felt she "… might as well go on the dole and become a drug dealer". This misunderstanding about the nature of entrepreneurs has remained a problem for us throughout the project, and for the people we have worked with. As if ambition only belongs to those who can afford it. As if entrepreneurship was just about business success rather than vision and flair. As if it could only be taught at business school.

Somewhere between Liverpool 8 and Liverpool 3 postal districts, the language of support changes. It is clear that there is little understanding or appreciation of the impact a different use of language, vocabulary or style can have. And of course, everyone who turns away from business advice with a bad experience will tell ten others not to go there. What price a formal enterprise culture then?

There are exceptions, of course. One of the most unexpected in Toxteth has been the Inland Revenue. Once the scariest people on the planet, they have moved mountains to improve their support for business. The Inland Revenue Business Support Team has spoken to my clients, with a sensitivity and appreciation for their circumstances that left them all with a positive feeling.

The trouble is that the current system is fixated on monitoring and not on people. It is just not possible to monitor and measure what is really important in regeneration to the community members themselves – emotions, culture, levels of trust, passion, circumstances, pride, fragility, ego, levels of respect. You have to get in, gain trust and credibility, and do what it takes to support people to move forward.

In practice, local people trading together in the formal economy build community cohesion and trust. If that starts to happen, then communication increases, crime drops and fear of crime begins to melt. Other things happen, too.

Laurence, a client, wants to convert an old pub on Lodge Lane into a café with space for musicians to play, as well as office space upstairs. He says, 'Lodge Lane still has a bit of vibrancy about it – although most of Toxteth is still suffering from the reputation of the riots. But if we could attract more small businesses to locate on Lodge Lane it would be great for regenerating the area. There are a lot of businesses in Toxteth but most of them work in isolation. That is why I want the café and the workspace to bring people together and be a meeting place for the community.'

Through BizFizz, Laurence has already found a network of talented people in this area, including an interior designer and a local filmmaker to produce a promotional video. The truth is that Liverpool 8 is actually full of entrepreneurs, and there is no shortage of passion and desire to achieve. Unleash this vibrant pool of life, and Liverpool will genuinely have its capital of culture. This tremendous creative force, below the radar of mainstream agencies, and dangerously subversive to many of them, is also overwhelmingly human.

I was asked once what one thing I would change to improve the prospects of budding entrepreneurs. I said that I would put more of the human back into the system, depend less of the processing of people, and adopt a coaching approach based in the heart of the community.

That is also the real meaning of being an entrepreneur, not the mythical drive for hyper-wealth the media has told us about. *'I don't want to be rich – I just want to provide stability for my daughter. Money doesn't matter that much to me. I just want the freedom of having my own business,'* said one of my clients. *'I have always been creative and I want to do what I am good at and do it well.'*

Being an entrepreneur is not really what we have been told by a generation of business school alumni. It is about imagination and humanity, and – although the official mind can be suspicious of such resources – these resources are there in abundance in Toxteth, as they are everywhere else.

Chapter 1
At the edge

Paul Squires

"A Good City is home to an above average number of entrepreneurs."

Bishop of Newcastle's Good City hearings, 2004

"If we receive funding next time, we'll know that our business support project has been a success."

Anonymous business advisor

"Nobody in their right mind could call me a Marxist," said Sir Richard O'Brien, chair of the Church of England committee that produced the ground-breaking *Faith in the City* report in 1985. He was responding to anonymous Government briefings warning that the report was going to be wildly and unfeasibly leftist. As it was, *Faith in the City* happened to coincide with another round of urban riots in England, including the destructive disturbance at Broadwater Farm in London, which served to underline the urgent need for radical solutions.

Faith in the City was not the first report to identify the need for business support for local entrepreneurs in places in need of regeneration, but it was the first to get the idea seriously onto the policy-making map. It made sense to all sides of the political divide, but what also came with it was a radical assumption that the regeneration industry had not so far grasped: that deprived neighbourhoods did, in fact, have a rather important resource at their disposal – local people and their drive and imagination.

The Church's report came three years before the Government's *Action for Cities*, the apotheosis of the idea that regeneration was about physical infrastructure not people – the fantasy that once a place like Salford Quays or the Isle of Dogs *looked* better, the job of regeneration was done. Despite this policy obsession with building your way out of deprivation, the need for business support had taken a small, but significant foothold in the policy landscape.

I was first involved in regeneration in the East Midlands at that time, and the grant money available was overwhelmingly about rebuilding. It was true that the rebuilding was aimed partly at underpinning the efforts of business people, to start up and employ people. It was for managed workspace, or small industrial units, in areas of high unemployment. In its own terms, this was a successful policy. The units were built and they were used. The trouble was that they were rarely used by anyone who actually lived there. Small businesses were starting up, and they were employing people, but these were mainly people from somewhere else who were gleeful at the prospect of cheap business accommodation.

In the following decade, with the introduction of Single Regeneration Budget (SRB) grants, there was an attempt to knit together the budgets for very different but equally vital funding streams. It was then possible to find funding for salaries, where appropriate, as well as buildings. The business support infrastructure was also gearing up. But there was an inherent weakness to SRB, which has still not been addressed by subsequent area regeneration programmes: they were driven by targets set by outside funders rather than reflecting the local context and local success criteria.

The difficulty, then and now, is that these funded, area-based programmes found themselves 'buying outputs' rather than delivering appropriate support. There is, in practice, a real tension between meeting targets and good practice in supporting new businesses starting-up, whether they are profit-making or social enterprises. This tension results in an uneasy reciprocal relationship, whereby funders cascade the money down the food chain of regeneration agencies, but they require outputs in return for the help they provide. There is often a major difference between these targets and outputs, and the aims of the practitioners in the organisations.

This tension is exacerbated by the problems of centralisation and nervousness about fraud. Governments have now introduced so many measures to stop fraud that the pressure on regeneration officials is always to look first at the financial implications of any support. They therefore tend to be risk averse which results in considerable sums left unspent at the end of any major programme. Then, to reach their required targets, they need to go out and find anyone who is likely to fulfil them – who may not be, and in fact are usually not, the people who would most benefit.

Bottom-up regeneration, the most powerful model of change, is impossible if the controlling strategy comes from distant funders requiring abstract outputs. Over the years of running BizFizz, we have found many committed business support professionals. But they are hamstrung by being driven by targets that are sometimes appropriate to their work, but more usually get frustratingly in the way of supporting their clients. They need to cling onto clients when it may not be in their interests. They need to prevent those clients seeking advice elsewhere, even when they need it – because that would lose the valuable outputs to which their funding is attached. BizFizz is a business coaching programme that avoids this fatal pitfall.

I first came across BizFizz when I was working in Birmingham. The Small Business Service had just agreed to fund four BizFizz pilot areas, via the Phoenix Development Fund. I was, at the time, working for a social enterprise development agency and I was finding it frustrating. Most of the people who wanted business support did not actually want to set up social enterprises. But we were funded only to help them do that, so all I could do was to point these entrepreneurs in other directions. Coming across BizFizz was a revelation to me. It was a process that gave both the advisors and their clients the freedom to be what they actually wanted to be. It was not about imposing a structure on people that never quite managed to fit them. Entrepreneurs would decide how to run their new business, whether it was going to be a social enterprise or not. At least they had the choice.

Having discovered the programme, it was only a matter of weeks later that a job came up at the Civic Trust which gave me the opportunity to work on BizFizz more directly. That was, for me, the beginning of an extraordinary journey to see what is really going on under the radar of regenerating neighbourhoods.

First and foremost, the inspiration behind BizFizz was E. F. Schumacher's book *Small is Beautiful.* There is no direct parallel to BizFizz anywhere in its pages, but the spirit of economics "as if people mattered", as he put it, is at the heart of the idea. Both are assertions that, if you get the small things right, then big things happen as a result.

That was the starting point. From Schumacher's approach to economics, a number of questions followed about conventional regeneration. Why, for example, are so few entrepreneurs coming forward in regenerating neighbourhoods, given the considerable amount of business support that is supposed to be available? After working for four years in Birmingham city centre, I knew that the percentage of small business start-ups was tiny compared to those emerging in more affluent suburbs just a few miles away.

There was another question, too. Given that imbalance, could we conclude that there really is no entrepreneurial spirit or behaviour in these rundown communities, because that was often what was inferred by policy-makers. Spending any time there should be enough to convince anyone this is not the case. Far from it. There is a great deal going on, some of it in the shadow economy – some of it actually criminal – but it is certainly entrepreneurial and takes considerable effort.

Then we had to ask: is there anyone out there who has found a way to tap into that energy and use it to regenerate communities?

The answer was yes. There were organisations like Five Lamps in Yorkshire, funded by Business Link to do outreach work in regenerating communities and advising people how to start a business. There were others like the Prince's Trust, which was pioneering the idea of using a 'panel' to support business start-ups. We also looked abroad and found innovative work in the USA, India and Australia.

Back in the UK, Bernie Ward and Mikyla Robinson – respectively working at **nef** and the Civic Trust – had discussed these conundrums and were looking for some kind of project that knitted these ideas together. Both their organisations were dedicated to looking at the kind of assets that economists tend to ignore when they evaluate regenerating neighbourhoods. These are, after all, communities that may not have much capital, but they have people and ideas and also a considerable combined spending power.

The Civic Trust had, and still has, a regeneration unit. The organisation as a whole dates back to 1958, and – even back then – the creeping realisation that physical regeneration can never work by itself without reference to the people who live there. Over and over again, we have some of the best urban architecture that money can buy, but because nothing is done to address or listen to the dreams and desires of the people who live there, the same levels of deprivation emerge again shortly afterwards. The height of this folly came with the slum clearances of the 1960s which simply decanted people to outlying estates and towers, breaking up what social networks of support existed before.

The Civic Trust was launched to support local amenity societies, and through this emerged a national policy that set out programmes of support for the people who lived in these regenerating neighbourhoods. One forerunner of BizFizz at the Civic Trust was a programme called Winning Partnerships, helping residents to learn how to develop effective partnerships with the public and private sector. We had a strong belief at this stage that networks of people were the key to regeneration programmes. BizFizz was a way of delivering business support locally that recognised this.

nef as an organisation has its foundations in The Other Economic Summits (TOES) in 1984 and 1985 – a critique of mainstream economics and its consequences. **nef**'s work focuses on the fundamental questions of how economic life could be organised differently. Central to that work is the recognition of social capital being at least as important as economic capital when it comes to regenerating a neighbourhood. Also that in places where these two kinds of assets intersect – the way that money flows around a local economy – can provide clues about hidden assets that economically disadvantaged neighbourhoods possess. Helping communities measure these money flows was a forerunner project that Bernie Ward developed at **nef** before BizFizz.

Bernie and Mikyla led the initial work. It was Bernie's idea to call the central organising tool of BizFizz 'business coaches'. The BizFizz title itself was suggested by Perry Walker, head of **nef**'s Centre for Participation, at a brainstorm held at the Civic Trust in 2001. The Phoenix Development Fund agreed to fund the development and piloting of the approach, and those involved found themselves learning a great deal about coaching methodology, and why it looked the best way of delivering any sort of advice. By then, BizFizz was based on a critique of conventional regeneration that recognised that it:

● Focused on investment in things and not in people. Capital programmes left a legacy of new buildings and facilities but still no reductions in underlying deprivation.

- Frequently helped set up community groups, drawing on some form of central funding, but overlooked the role of individual entrepreneurship as a driver for regeneration.

- Geared support towards the achievement of central aims of commercial growth rather than on the needs of aspiring entrepreneurs.

- Tended to undermine the value of support being given by setting inappropriate targets for support programmes.

In response, BizFizz was developed as a programme that could flexibly operate within defined communities, usually of around 8,000 to 15,000 people. It was vital that the local community identified the opportunity that BizFizz brought to them, decided to be part of the programme, and organised themselves to host it locally. That local organisation would include:

- A local management group (LMG), a small team which was to be responsible for helping to address any strategic or institutional barriers identified through the coach's work with clients – leaving the coach free to focus on clients and not get involved in committees. The LMG was to include a local resident, representatives of local agencies, the local authority and other partners, and members of the local business community. The coach was to keep the LMG informed of the real issues facing small businesses, helping it to deal with some of the strategic issues.

- A local panel which would be a much larger body (30–40 people), including entrepreneurs, residents, professionals and anyone else who the coach felt would add value. They were to be volunteers who would meet every month or two to act as a problem-solving panel for individual business cases brought to them by the coach. Through their contacts, their local knowledge, and their links in the community, they would begin to find ways that individual entrepreneurs could overcome barriers standing in the way of their success.

The idea was that BizFizz coaches, who would be entrepreneurs themselves, would be at the heart of that community, making contact with local groups and representatives, helping to put people in contact with each other, letting potential entrepreneurs know that they were there if needed, and then being available to meet them at times, places, frequencies and circumstances suitable to the clients.

The time had come to launch the programme. We had attracted applications to be pilot areas from 25 different places. We sent a small team out to visit them, and prepared a SWOT analysis, reflecting details included in the applications as the basis for that conversation. Even this turned out to be controversial. On more than one occasion, we were shouted at by passionate residents who regarded our SWOT analysis as deeply insulting.

By the end of this process, we were prepared to launch in four areas. They included Horden and Easington in Durham, a former coal mining area on the coast, and Tuxford in north Nottinghamshire, a small market town and the few villages around it. We chose another market town, Thetford in Norfolk, and the former shipbuilding town of Jarrow. We also began interviewing our panel members.

Our initial thinking was that we wanted a panel to provide solutions to the problems entrepreneurs would have, and a perfect example of how this was supposed to work came up almost immediately in Tuxford. We were helping a local ceramics business, which made replica pots for museums. But they were based outside Tuxford and wanted a shop on the high street so they could showcase other products. A quick chat with the local estate agent ascertained immediately that there was no property available. We brought the problem up at the very first panel meeting.

There was a local farmer at the meeting, who said he had a barn right in the middle of Tuxford, which he used to store rusty machinery. The BizFizz coach Fred Foreshaw then worked with the farmer to help him arrange to make the building useable, and brokered an arrangement so the company could use it.

I thought that was a beautifully elegant example of how the panel should work. The farmer had no direct reason for being on the panel other than a passion for Tuxford, and wanting to do something to help. He wasn't part of the great and the good, it wasn't his job, and he did not represent a voluntary organisation. He simply agreed to give two hours of his time to the panel, and as a result, a small but significant change happened. The resources of the town were also better used.

The panels quickly became a central component for a whole new way of organising regeneration. BizFizz was beginning to emerge as an idea with some radical propositions at its heart, which upset some accepted notions. For example:

Just providing advice undermines potential entrepreneurs
Conventional business advice services have a central problem, which is that because they only have recourse to certain solutions they are often hamstrung by their official agenda. Business Link, for example, can suggest that a client goes on a training course, and that might be very useful for some people. But there are many reasons why that might not be appropriate for everyone. The needs of aspiring entrepreneurs can be diverse, so it is vital that that we did not simply say: "Well, thanks for telling me that. Now, what we normally recommend to people starting out in business is ..." One of the benefits of coaching is that the client–coach relationship is led by the client, and goes wherever the client needs to take it. BizFizz coaches have come to talk more recently about how they 'hold the client's agenda', just as the panels hold a BizFizz agenda in the local community. The coaching process is designed to identify and draw out where the entrepreneur is strong, and what they are passionate about.

Funding targets support the funder at the expense of their effect on the ground
Business support that is driven by fulfilling targets is focused on fulfilling those targets, rather than meeting the individual needs of clients – whatever they happen to be. These targets are embedded in the payment system for New Deal for Self-Employment, for example, which protects the benefits of new entrepreneurs for six months, takes any other earnings and gives them back to you the day you come off benefits. Payment for the agency also comes when the business starts. There is enormous pressure because of this, on the client and advisor, to launch a new business whether it is appropriate or sustainable or not.

Being an entrepreneur is not about ploughing a lonely furrow
All our evidence suggests that social networks, and embedding entrepreneurs in them, leads to much wider and more successful entrepreneurial activity. We have become used to the idea of entrepreneurs as heroic individualists, when actually most successful entrepreneurs are primarily brilliant networkers: the difference between success and failure is probably the networks of local people who can help them. Recent research in the east of England also confirms that successful

single parents, bringing up children and holding down a job, manage it because they are supported by very good networks. BizFizz was therefore designed around a panel that provides access to local networks. The panel members also provide a temporary team around the entrepreneur, filling gaps in their skills or knowledge. At the beginning, coaches would be in the middle of this network, but would hopefully become increasingly peripheral to them as they developed further.

Promotion and marketing distort the regeneration process

We agreed at the outset that coaches would work without doing the kind of promotion that is considered ubiquitous in business advice programmes. Coaches would have to find canny ways of getting known through word of mouth – and one route might be to get panel members to refer people they knew. But if networks make the difference between success and failure, then reaching over the heads of those networks to persuade people that they wanted to set up a business – and that they also badly needed advice – was counter-productive. The process of spreading the word would have to support the networks that were so badly needed.

The first hurdles to cross were about convincing funders that these heresies were worth risking in practice. We insisted to our funders, the Phoenix Development Fund and Small Business Service, that we would accept no targets, and were delighted when they agreed almost immediately – influenced at the time by the Policy Action Team report (PAT 17) from the Social Exclusion Unit that outcomes were more important than targets. It has sometimes been more difficult to persuade some of the coaches, some of whom found that it was a struggle to start with if they had no set numerical goals. But, two years into the job, I believe they vowed not to go anywhere near a target again.

We found we were testing some of our propositions almost instinctively. There was no conventional job description for a business coach, for example, because there was no such thing – in regeneration at least. There was also the problem of how we were going to train them. They were far more experienced about business advice than we were, so we could hardly tell them how to do the job in the usual way. We hoped instead we could encourage them to think about the task ahead in new ways, and looked around for an organisation that might help us.

We found the solution in a very unexpected place: relationship guidance. Relate North East was a regional branch of the national service for relationship guidance counselling, and they had begun to do some training of business advisors in counselling skills. We hired them to help us and they ran a coaching training session in Nottingham. Most of what we all learned there was the theoretical aspects of being Relate counsellors.

Looking back, the Nottingham training was enormous fun. We looked at transactional analysis, as well as at bereavement and other counselling skills – listening, summarising and reflecting. But more importantly, there was something about the power of self-reflection that people in their normal work rarely have the opportunity to do – we are not normally encouraged to do it at work. Once you start that process, it can be very powerful. It made us, I believe, constantly curious about clients. I also think it encouraged us to take the necessary risks that made BizFizz such a success.

We were also meeting together for the first time, staying in an almost empty Nottingham hotel. On the second night, we went out to the Old Trip to Jerusalem pub, the inn from where the crusaders set out to Palestine in 1190. In the minibus taxi on the way back, the driver said: "You don't want to stay there – that hotel's been closed for six months after one of the guests died of Legionnaires Disease."

It is possible to imagine a whole range of significant icebreakers, but there is nothing as good as shared terror – it closed permanently a few months later.

Over that weekend, we found we had employed four extraordinary people as coaches. There was the Horden coach, Elliott Patterson, who had been in training development. There was Tuxford's Fred Forshaw, a former consultant engineer. For Thetford, we chose Alison Ball, who had worked for Business Link and had worked in a print co-op. In Jarrow, we chose Keith Jeffrey, who had been working for the National Glass Museum in the north-east. They were all interesting, dynamic self-starters, who would probably describe themselves as mavericks. They certainly gave us a hard time by pushing at the boundaries of what we were hoping to achieve, and were as curious as we were about what was possible. They were all four really passionate about business support and all keen to have the freedom to do things in new ways. They did not, for example, set out immediately in the same direction. I know Fred spent much of first few months working with existing businesses, while Keith concentrated on younger people who had never set up in business before.

Then we ran into the first operational difficulties. In the first panel meetings the discussion was very theoretical to start with. Our intention was that there should be at least 30 people: a third business advisors, a third from the local great and good, and a third entrepreneurs and residents. Sure enough, at the first panel meeting in Jarrow, six business advisors turned up.

The first client case in front of the panel was a 19-year-old who wanted to set up an IT networking business, and who had a marketing question. The business advisors started immediately, not with an answer to this question, but with conventional advisor questions: How old is he? Has he got enough cashflow? Can we see a marketing strategy? As the discussion continued, they got increasingly exasperated, because they were not getting their questions answered, any more than the client was. Then one member of the panel stood ostentatiously in the middle of the room, and said that BizFizz should not be dealing with this client at all. "We deal with 19-year-olds," he said, referring to his own business advice service.

This convinced us of one lesson at least. We could only have one business advisor on the panels and that was the coach. Other advisors would only be invited if they were really passionate about both BizFizz and the area. We uninvited them, and explained the difference in our approach. They were driven by targets; we were not. They were seeking information for themselves to reinforce their own models of how a business should be run – we wanted information to help clients inform their own learning about their business.

This quickly emerged as a bigger difference than we had imagined. Elliott was contacted by a man who had been convinced to start a painting and decorating business, and had been sent by conventional business advisors on a test-trading course for three months. This was strange to start with: you can do a business plan for that kind of business in a day – what painters and decorators need is to get out and find a market. Given this, he was finding the course soul-destroying.

But when Elliott eventually asked the trainee painter and decorator what he was passionate about it, he said it wasn't decorating at all. He was doing that in order to get £1,000 so that he could get a licence to be a hang-gliding instructor. Elliott's next question was: "If I can find £1,000 for you, what would you do?"

"Set up a hand gliding school", he said. Brilliant! Elliott's question gave the man an opportunity to forget his immediate concerns – his reality – and step in to the future, and then share for the first time his true passion.

That one story, so early in the whole programme, demonstrated to us the power of coaching, and why target-driven business advice means that the motivation comes from the advisor and not the entrepreneur. It was clear that we needed to investigate the mechanics and the possibilities of coaching further, and we did so.

Another founding principle of BizFizz was becoming clearer, too: energy and passion made things happen, and the energy from people finding ways of doing what they were passionate about was infectious.

A little later, at another panel meeting in Jarrow, I met someone from the Inland Revenue, and I asked her why she came. She said the main reason was that she came from Jarrow herself, and she enormously enjoyed spending two hours on a Friday evening every so often helping people from there. It was, in a way, passion about a place that was motivating her, and these things are infectious, too, in a way that meeting targets are not. Passion was what drew together the entrepreneurs and the panel members, and gave them something in common.

That passion provided a commitment to really get to the bottom of why clients were there. The hang-gliding story was repeated in so many other ways, as we discovered increasingly that what people really needed was not something that fit easily onto a list of official outputs. One client with plans for a mobile cleaning business actually needed coaching for himself and his wife to help them agree if this was a sensible move from the family's perspective. Another client visited twice a week with small enquiries before feeling comfortable enough to discuss his large debts and the fact that his business was a big factor in restoring his self-esteem. Each of them required a very different approach to be taken, and we had adopted a system that provided the flexibility to do this.

As the new businesses moved through their various stages of development, coaches could help where they were needed, whether that was market research, business planning, cash flow forecasting, marketing plans, risk analysis, seeking finance, rules and regulations, HR planning, and so on. But with BizFizz, the relationship can and does develop in unexpected directions, and coaches find themselves helping in quite curious ways:

- Staffing the client's mobile food wagon for a couple of hours while the client meets with a possible corporate customer.

- Meeting builders at a client's shop premises, enabling them to do quotes, while the client looked after his market stall.

- Driving a finance application around to get appropriate signatures in order to meet a tight deadline.

- Acting as an intermediary between a shopkeeper and a recalcitrant landlord.

- Negotiating deferred terms on a new business premises.

- Taking an aspiring retailer around the nearby shopping centre to get the feel for what the competition was like.

Conventional business advisors might say that none of these was their job, but in all those cases, that small piece of practical help made a fundamental difference to that entrepreneur's future.

By the time we reached the second phase of the programme, we were working with a much more defined model. In 2004, the programme was extended to cover eight more communities: Ocean Estate (east London), Bowthorpe (Norwich), Winsford (Cheshire), Alnwick (Northumberland), Belgrave (Leicester), Toxteth (Liverpool), Stanley Green Corridor (County Durham), and Clowne (North Derbyshire). This second phase also received some support from the Phoenix Development Fund, but was mainly financed by local sources of funding. BizFizz projects are now being commissioned in various communities around the country, using a variety of local funding sources.

Each of the BizFizz communities is very different in their geography, culture, existing commerce, levels of wealth and deprivation, and the types of other organisations already working within the area. Each of the projects reflects the development context it sits within, and the outcomes of each project are determined by local context. Towards the end of the pilot phase I heard a number of policy-makers suggest some BizFizz pilots had failed as the other ones had managed a larger number of business start-ups over the pilot lifetime. I believe that without understanding local context, using outputs as a comparator to work out who succeeded and who failed is pretty meaningless.

In response to this, we invited members of the local management groups of second phase programmes to name their local success criteria. In Clowne, the local management group felt that if half the shops on the high street were run by local entrepreneurs, the programme would be successful. In Winsford, they wanted to measure the impact of the programme in neighbourhoods that, according to the local social services, were 'undergoing family stress'. Also Gary, the local management group chair, said that he would know the programme worked if someone walked up to him in the street and told him that BizFizz had changed his life. This happened eighteen months into the programme.

The real battle with BizFizz has been around redefining the concept of entrepreneur. When we first did a presentation about entrepreneurship and passion, we found that people understood what we were trying to say about the central importance of passion very quickly. But the word 'entrepreneur' continued to bug people. People in the voluntary sector preferred the word 'enterprise'. Others assumed you were talking about the owner of a national or multinational business. We believe that it isn't a person or a thing; it's an attitude.

Most surveys confirm that about 20 to 22 per cent of the adult population have entrepreneurial attitudes. They are interested in selling things or making things happen. The truth is that this sense is not about a few individuals, or confined to middle class suburbs: you will find entrepreneurial activity everywhere – including the informal economy. Once people realise they are not expected to behave like Alan Sugar – then they can start doing something.

I believe that coaching methodology is the best way to deliver business support to entrepreneurs living in the communities we work with. Over the last twenty years, business support has been offered in the communities we wanted to work in and we noticed that economic decline in these communities had not been reversed, and in many cases had gotten worse. There was no doubt that business support agencies employed advisors who had knowledge and expertise; what we challenged was assumptions about how that advice was offered to entrepreneurs. There are accreditation awards for business advisors that test their competencies and institutions that form policy and develop standards for business advice. What became apparent was that these institutions and awards concentrated on what the advisor knew, not on how they offered the knowledge they had to clients.

There is no particular set method: coaches choose to work with methodologies that suit them. We offer new coaches the over-arching principles of coaching to inform their practice and to tease out the differences between coaching, advising, mentoring and counselling and then invite them to investigate and practice a coaching methodology of their choice.

At a conference in 2005, Sue Stockdale – author of a book called *Kickstart your Motivation* – told the story of a team of mixed-experience Arctic explorers. The slowest skier was put at the front of the line, with the most experienced behind her. Heading through dangerous crevasses, he shouted his instructions ahead to her. In frustration and anger, she turned and asked him to stop yelling orders, and to tell her instead what he would be looking for if he were leading the line. She wanted to learn for herself. They then agreed that if he saw something she'd missed, he would shout 'STOP', and ask her questions that would enable her to see this potential danger for herself. This is an excellent analogy for business coaching. It's not enough if the business advisor just gives out instructions; they are not even in the crevasse with you! Running a business requires fast learning for the entrepreneur – about themselves, their business, the market environment and everything that will impact on them as they get deeper into their chosen territory.

In this book, we share our learning about the values and components of BizFizz, the relationships between funders and institutions, business support agencies and clients, coaches and entrepreneurs and offer stories about the resourceful and passionate people we met in communities labelled by others as 'disadvantaged and deprived'. There is also in the book an underlying discussion about power; who has it and who doesn't and how this affects the delivery of business support in the communities we work in.

We say that BizFizz is a client-focused process, that any decision taken by a coach, panel members, institutions and the national team, is informed by the question: "Does the client benefit?" We believe that entrepreneurs find power within themselves and express this through their passion and energy to start and grow businesses; they are not empowered, rescued or created by anyone else. And yet common practice in advising is often the complete opposite of this. We have seen and heard advisors talking about motivating their clients or getting them to perform. I heard one advisor explain how it took him six months to convince a client to become a photographer. "I got him in the end," he said.

This need to put another notch on the bedpost tells us as much about the institution that employed him as an advisor as it does about him and where and how power is used. An advising relationship can lead to dependency when an advisor 'lends' their energy to a client so that they perform for, and are motivated by the advisor. In this type of relationship, advisors are using their expertise to lead the client's business development, which denies the opportunity for a client to learn. When the advising relationship ends, which in the current climate of business support rationing it does pretty quickly, the major driver of the business idea leaves. Then what the entrepreneur is left with is the knowledge of how another person would run their business.

We believe that the entrepreneur has sole responsibility for the business, that it is their passion that drives it, and that they must have the opportunity to learn about their business and about themselves. Which is why, in any stage of business development or growth, we ask: "who's the entrepreneur?"

Interlude: Nostalgia Designs, Alnwick

"I'd been ill, and wanted to return to work but needed a flexible job. My husband designs wedding dresses – so we turned a 25-year hobby into a reality. We refurbished the shop and brought it into the 21st century. It's been the right thing to do, and it's well accepted in the locality. I'm happy, and everyone's so excited when they come to the shop!

I called the local BizFizz coach, Mark, when I heard about him in an interior design shop – the owner is on the BizFizz panel. I'd been trawling business advisers and it was Mark's approach that appealed – he's natural, and he treated me seriously. Not all of the others did that. He believed I could do it and he offers practical help.

I tell everyone about Mark and BizFizz because it's great. If something goes wrong, Mark looks at it in a different way. He looks at the downside as an opportunity."

Joan Orr

Chapter 2
Trust

Anne Francis

*"I have three business advisors, but you are the real one –
I only go to the others for the money."*
BizFizz client, Ocean Estate, East London

"Trust the tale."
D. H. Lawrence

Shortly after I began work as the BizFizz coach for Bowthorpe in Norfolk, a new client came to see me who wanted to start up a customised clothing and vintage jewellery retail business. I was impressed with her. She used to work as a buyer for a major fashion retailer, so she knew the industry well. She was also a single mother, with a nine-month-old baby, who had recently moved into the area.

It was clear to me right from the start that Jane had an enormous passion for her venture. This was just as well because she had been told by the Job Centre Plus officials not to bother starting up a business. They told her she would have to make at least £16,000 to make it worth her while coming off benefits, and advised that it was much better to wait until her child was five years old and off to school before going into self-employment. This wasn't going to stop Jane: this business was her dream. She wanted a better life for herself and her daughter and that meant being her own boss.

She was so enthusiastic when I first met her that I just let her talk and tell me all about her plans. She presented a few practical barriers she was facing, as well as some internal barriers, such as lack of confidence. As a BizFizz coach, I look at the client as a whole person, not just the business in isolation. So we worked on overcoming personal as well as external barriers.

Jane had started on the government's Test Trading programme which gives you a six-month period where you can start up your business and still receive benefits. The trouble was that she was finding that the agency sub-contracted by Job Centre Plus to run the programme was very restrictive, inflexible and overly bureaucratic. She had to go for regular fixed appointments at 2pm every fortnight in Norwich, which really broke up her day and caused problems with childcare. The advice given at those appointments was very superficial and impersonal: as far as Jane could see, they had specific duties they had to perform to meet their targets, but it was hard to imagine that they were really interested in their client's business.

On one occasion, Jane had to cancel an appointment because she had to take her daughter to the doctor. They said that next time she had to change an appointment, she would be thrown off the Test Trading programme. Another time, on the morning of a meeting with her first potential buyer, her Test Trading mentor phoned up and said that if she failed to get a contract with the buyer, she would be taken off the scheme. She already felt nervous enough about meeting this buyer, but this ratcheted up the pressure so much that it threatened the success of the meeting. It was not in her nature to burst into tears easily, but this is what she did. But it felt like an ultimatum because that was what it was.

The problem was not just the targets which governed the work of the Test Trading agency. Jane felt that their advisors did not understand her, or her business or her long term ambition and game plan. Nor did they try. They seemed to believe that anyone Test Trading was simply messing around. There was a deep-seated belief that their clients were timewasters and were not to be trusted.

Test Trading has been an important prop for entrepreneurs, and it is a backward step that it has since been made even more forbidding and bureaucratic. But there was another problem with Test Trading for Jane: in order to get around legislation which makes earning income while in receipt of benefits illegal, the agency takes control over the client's cheque book.

Of course, I can understand they need to keep an eye on clients' bank accounts, but it makes it very difficult dealing with suppliers. If Jane wanted to buy anything – even a £7 item – she had to phone the Test Trading agency and ask them to raise a cheque, which then had to be signed by two people. They would then send the cheque by post to Jane and only then could she can send the cheque on to the supplier. This is not only time-consuming, it is also embarrassing. Also, if a buyer paid Jane, they had to write the cheque to TFS Trading, which is the Test Trading account, rather than her business name. This goes down like a lead balloon with clients. It feels unprofessional, and forces her to explain that she is actually on benefits.

This approach may have provided clear management reports. It may have ticked plenty of boxes and hit the targets, but it created further barriers to success for Jane.

Perhaps it sounds a little naïve to suggest that they should have trusted anyone. I have no doubt that the systems were designed with a healthy regard for the importance of public money. The point is that, without a trusting relationship between entrepreneur and advisor, very little is possible. If the agency is so big and so hidebound by systems and checklists that it is unable to generate that relationship, then it will be ineffective. And that makes the waste of public money even more disturbing. Because the whole purpose of the agency was to help entrepreneurs set up, so the lack of trust between the agency and the client provided fundamental barriers to the progress of Jane's business.

Talking to policy-makers, you might imagine there was no other way to do it – that it was impossible to design an advice system that provided genuine support based on trust. But that was what BizFizz set out to do, and the trust has to go both ways. That is what a coaching relationship can provide, and the enormous success of BizFizz shows that such things are possible.

Each time Jane faced a new barrier, we talked it through and I learned to trust that she had the knowledge, resources and determination to overcome it. I would ask her questions like "why do you think you can't do that?" or "what exactly is stopping you?" Each time, Jane found a way out of the difficult situations. Her confidence grew and even in really stressful situations, she didn't give up.

There were a couple of times when she came up against an unexpected brick wall, for example when she was due at a trade show and her childcare fell through. At that stage, the support she really needed was emergency childcare, so I took care of her baby for two hours. Another time, she gave me the keys to her house so I could let in someone to repair her sewing machine while she had to go to the Test Trading meeting.

I believe that, between us, we built up a huge amount of trust – but the agenda was always in Jane's hands. She was the driver. She had the energy and passion. I just persisted in supporting her to remove the barriers, and working with her taught me a great deal. It showed me the importance of listening to what clients already know, taking my cues from them and having absolute confidence that they know what they are doing.

But it also taught me the central importance of trust, and I saw the same issue – lack of trust – over and over again in government-funded business support. Across the BizFizz projects, we have come across many institutions, purportedly set up to support businesses, which place yet more bureaucratic barriers in the way. These institutions are focused on their own needs, rather than on those of the clients. They allow administrative systems to dominate their delivery – to the extent that they process clients rather than enabling them to express their passions. They take the people out of business.

After waiting seven weeks for an appointment with a business support agency, a client in East London was simply given an application form requiring a business plan in a particular format. The agency would not release the format in advance, so that the client could attend the first meeting prepared. And they had their personal data taken down to log outputs. After being admitted to hospital, another client in Derbyshire was told this discontinuity meant he could no longer be considered part of the Test Trading scheme.

If you imagine people taking their first tentative steps into business on their own, the bizarre way that the institutions that are supposed to help end up hindering them can take your breath away. When one BizFizz client's loan was approved, the loan manager in Norfolk put it on hold, because it had been approved too quickly. And following two months on the Test Trading scheme, another client was told that her financial records were not acceptable – because she had used the wrong brand of accounting book.

There is no doubt that the data collection requirements of some funders and the performance management systems of business support institutions can and do create barriers to entrepreneurial success. They do not understand the needs of entrepreneurs in disadvantaged areas, and the result is a kind of collusion between funders and agencies which only benefits themselves. They also serve to restrict the freedom of advisors to do their job, because the institutions are not set up to trust them either. There is no recognition that advisors can be self-driven; that they are dedicated, and have a passion for what they do.

That is how BizFizz is different. We start with a simple question: what does an entrepreneur want? Targets and outcomes are not the motivation for a BizFizz coach. The energy in the relationship comes from the entrepreneur, from their passion for what they want to do. The coach is there to help remove the barriers that stand in their way. That means building a relationship of trust out of which exciting things can happen. Trust is really central.

The importance of trust was drummed into us new coaches at the BizFizz induction week in Spring 2004 after I joined. That was the point where all the new coaches gathered together before we were dispatched to work in different communities around the country. We were told that, first and foremost, we would need to trust that the people we were going to work with had all the knowledge and resources they needed. They had the answers, not us. We were not the experts.

I must say, I certainly didn't feel like an expert. In fact, at that stage, I felt like a bit of an impostor. I had previously worked for a business support organisation, worked in micro-finance, set up an enterprise network and run my own crèche business across Norfolk employing twelve people. Even so, I knew that being a BizFizz coach was going to be a real challenge. This was not a traditional business support service, with fixed appointments and clear targets. As BizFizz coaches, we were tasked with 'hanging out' in the community and told to see what happens. To ask if there was anybody there who wanted to do something. I was exhilarated to get the job, but a little unsure about what to expect.

I arrived to work as a BizFizz coach in Bowthorpe in June 2004. Bowthorpe is a ward in the city of Norwich. The council bought the land in the 1960s to provide a small 'new town' with housing and employment. Nearly half a century on, the area consists of three communities: Cloverhill, Chapel Break and Three Score, which are essentially residential housing estates, isolated from the rest of Norwich.

I had been there before. But as I arrived to take up my job, the area seemed particularly quiet. There was not even a high street. In fact, as

I walked around, I could hear the signpost from an abandoned pub creaking. I took stock of the area. There were a number of boarded-up shops and there seemed to be very little in the way of visible entrepreneurial activity. There was a small shopping centre with an independent supermarket called Roy's, as well as some chain stores. There was also an industrial estate where the businesses included Parcel Force and Kettle Foods, which is the area's largest employer.

So there I was on day one of my job. Where should I start? With no targets, no checklists and no agenda apart from listening and talking, this was no conventional assignment. I decided my first task was to get out and try and meet people, get my face known and start to build up some of this crucial trust in the community. I knew a number of people in the city and neighbouring wards, so although I knew few people in Bowthorpe, I felt fairly confident that I could start to make some good contacts. I started at the community centre, and I explained what I was trying to do, and got a discouraging response. "You won't find any entrepreneurs in Bowthorpe," they said. "It's not that sort of place."

I gulped a bit. I had to admit that it did feel a bit like a ghost town. My new office was also just outside the community in a first-floor room that was only accessible by ringing the buzzer downstairs. So I was not exactly going to get any drop-ins. Still, this was all the more reason to spend as much time out of the office as possible.

One of the key BizFizz principles that was drilled into us during the induction week was 'No Promotion'. We were not supposed so much as to produce flyers, leaflets, posters or adverts for the BizFizz service. We could have business cards, but that was it. Otherwise I just had to rely on the power of word-of-mouth recommendation.

So rather than making glossy promises through promotional material, I had to get to know people in the community, and to build up my own credibility. After all, people who would not normally visit a business coach if they saw it advertised on a poster, might come along if they heard about the service from a friend or someone in the community. That was the theory anyway, and I was determined to stick to it.

I had a very supportive local management group of four. Peter was an active member of the community who also runs Just Jive dance classes. There was Sharon from the city council, which were among the funders for the project. There was also Ian from the West Norwich Partnership who hosted me in their office and Nigel from Business Link in Norwich. The group acted as a sounding board but effectively had a very hands-off management approach. They trusted me to get on with the job according to the BizFizz model and if I needed any help, I knew I could ask them.

We met monthly when I reported on activities, but other than that, there were no outputs to meet. I found this was liberating. It was an absolute luxury to be able to operate without any bureaucratic restraints. But I struggled a little to find ways to reassure myself that I was doing the right things. With no external targets to measure my own success, I have had to really learn how to trust myself that I am doing a good job. Once again, it is trust that makes things possible. They learn to trust me and I have to learn to trust myself. Neither of those emerge automatically, and without any foundation. But in practice, human beings are able to make fine and effective judgements about other people – and about themselves – and do so every day without the aid of target measurements, which may or may not be relevant.

Peter made himself especially helpful by taking me around the community and introducing me to people. I'm not sure he knew quite what to make of me in the beginning, but he was passionate about the BizFizz approach and was a very effective advocate for it when he told people all about the programme.

In the first day, I also knocked on the door of the white goods repair shop, but they did not seem very interested in talking to the BizFizz coach. I also walked around the industrial estate. For some reason, I was expecting this to be the local hub of entrepreneurial activity. Actually, it was mainly uninviting offices for insurance or distribution companies. They had little or no involvement in the rest of Bowthorpe and were still detached from the community.

The one exception was Kettle Foods, who remain very responsive. Their community liaison officer agreed to join the BizFizz panel and another person offered his help to any individual clients that might need marketing advice. I made sure I visited all the main networking and community events and always gave people two of my business cards. The only thing I asked for was for people to tell other people about BizFizz and spread the crucial message by word of mouth.

By the end of June, after a few weeks on the job, I had two clients. For the first session, I read up on the notes I had made during the induction week and drew up a checklist of all the things I wanted to remember to say. I wanted to remember to tell them that it was a free service, that it was confidential and flexible. I wanted to make sure they knew they could call any time and, most importantly, that the agenda was theirs not mine. "It's entirely up to you as the client," I wanted to say, "what steps you want to take."

I knew this was the right thing to do in theory. But in the early days of the job, I could not stop myself providing them with as much information as possible. Looking back now, I probably swamped those clients in the first sessions with too many contacts, websites, pieces of information, events and heaven knows what else. So, although I knew it was impossible for me to understand their business, their passion and their values more than they did, I found it difficult to let go of the need to provide piles of useful information.

Despite this avalanche of information, my initial networking started to pay off and I soon had a flurry of new clients. So many that, after a couple of months, I began to feel rather overwhelmed. It was as if I was starting up twelve businesses at once. It felt like I was sharing a great deal of responsibility, because some of my clients were preparing to take risks to finance their businesses. I was terrified on their behalf. I soon realised that I simply had to let go and give up some of the responsibility. I am only responsible for myself and if I follow the BizFizz principle of trusting the clients, then I had to stop feeling as if I had to protect them from the risk of failure.

Another core value of the BizFizz coaching approach is 'never initiate, never motivate'. This might sound strange at first, because some people imagine that coaching is primarily about motivating people – and some forms of performance coaching can be. Yet as a BizFizz coach, I learnt to always ask 'Who is the entrepreneur?' This was to make sure that, as a coach, I did not slip into the role of the driving force behind the business. Or worse, that I was not the reason the business was being set up in the first place. Successful entrepreneurs are always passionate about their business. If had to motivate a client into starting a business, it would almost certainly fail.

Six months into the project, I had 17 clients. It still seemed fairly quiet, but I resisted the temptation to produce leaflets and posters. I just persisted with networking as much as possible. I had to trust that word of mouth was the best route to promoting myself in this community. Patience, patience, I told myself.

I started to be a little more challenging towards some of my clients. My background training was in a person-centred approach. This meant that whatever the client said or thought was fine – it came from them and that was their perspective and was all supposed to be valid. But increasingly, as I listened to them, I felt I was being too passive. Sometimes I had a real niggling feeling about something when a client was talking, and I took the risk to start naming this niggling feeling out loud.

One client, who was very bright and entrepreneurial, seemed to have an internal saboteur who kept telling her 'you can't do this or that'. It was almost as if a part of her was trying to keep her safe and stop her from taking risks. I challenged her by pointing out that she had a conscious choice: she could decide to do something or decide not to do something. But if she decided not to, that was a perfectly valid choice – and it was open to her. She could identify the barrier that was stopping her and then decide whether or not she wanted to do something about it. This seemed to make a huge difference and the client moved her business idea forward in great strides. I felt I had done the right thing.

Another client kept using anecdotes from the past to deflect issues. I felt that she was using these stories as excuses for what was really holding her back. As soon as I said this in the session, our conversation went to a much deeper level. She was rather shocked that I had said it, but by then she trusted me enough to want to explore it further.

I think the key is that, as a BizFizz coach, I am only interested in the client's agenda. I have no vested interest in wanting the client to start up so I can reach my targets. Nor am I an expert, an advisor or a parent figure. I can and should be detached enough from the outcome to give me absolute freedom to support clients to do whatever they want to do. I need to help people realise that they can actually take control of their lives. Trust makes that possible.

In my initial intake sessions now, I first ask the client for permission to challenge them. I tell them that I will be very straightforward, and that sometimes I will say things that they might not like. People always agree because this is what they want: someone to be honest, frank and open with them. That means I need to find another kind of trust in myself: I need to be able to trust my own intuition. If I do that, and I think there is something that a client is not saying or is even trying to hide – possibly from themselves – then I will ask them about it. Nine times out of ten, this takes the conversation to a much deeper and more productive level.

There are other ways that trust becomes important. Several times, clients have asked me to sit in on negotiations with funding partners or prospective landlords, to have someone they trust as an independent pair of eyes and ears. I once helped negotiate on behalf of a client who was starting a social enterprise working with children. Instead of suggesting a figure for how much grant we had in mind, I asked what they had in mind. They offered three times as much. I stayed very calm and said: "That sounds reasonable." It was very satisfying.

Another client was facing a huge barrier opening a business bank account because she had a blacklisted credit record. I did some research and phoned my contacts in the banks to see if any of them would consider her case on an individual basis or if they just had a blanket policy. The only bank that agreed to see her was Barclays, so we went together to see their small business account manager. My client said she felt more confident being able to take her business coach along. The bank manager was young and open-minded and so, early on in the meeting, we built up a good rapport between us. The meeting lasted over an hour and a half, but by the end he had agreed to give my client a bank account on a six-month trial basis. If all went well, he would then negotiate an extension of the free business banking after the first year and an overdraft facility. He also bought one of my client's products: not only a friendly bank manager but a new customer, too.

As well as helping clients to remove barriers, I also support them to build temporary teams. One person will never be good at everything, so where there is a gap for example in book-keeping skills or PR skills, I put clients in touch with people on the BizFizz panel or in the wider network. Clients have said that this has not only given them access to other important skills, but a real boost in confidence when other people in the community are prepared to support them in their business.

When Jane said that she wanted to hold a fashion show to promote her clothing designs, I put her in touch with some other clients to be models, take photographs, provide music or help with marketing. Several of the panel members also came along to support the event and the *Eastern Daily Press* and *Norwich Evening News* covered the story in the paper. It was really hard work for Jane, but turned out to be an enormous success. She has done several fashion shows since and is going from strength to strength.

Nine months into the project, there really seemed to be something of a buzz starting in Bowthorpe. The woman who had originally told me that I wouldn't find any entrepreneurs in Bowthorpe knocked on my door with a business idea of her own. I suddenly had a stream of new clients who had been referred by other clients.

The network is still fizzing. I have been working with a couple who worked in the airline industry to set up their own airline charter company, now up and running as F1 Air Charter Ltd. What they really needed was some good publicity, and through the BizFizz panel they have managed to find that. I have been working with a shoe designer, who had trained as a shoemaker in Africa but was working as a nurse. He had a dream to run a business doing bespoke shoe design for people with disabilities. Through BizFizz, he found funding and premises, and we even helped negotiate seven months' free rent. I originally asked for nine months in the meeting, and – although they all looked very shocked – they came back with an offer of seven.

Last week, I put out a very unusual request by email on behalf of a client who was looking for a Tamil speaker and someone who had experience in exporting to South India. This is a tricky request for a suburb of Norwich, but within half an hour, I had a personal contact sent to me for a Tamil speaker who also exported to South India.

A client-to-client peer support group has been established which meets every month in the local café. Both business editors on the city newspapers are very interested in BizFizz and are always keen to promote new businesses. Even the local MP Charles Clarke came to meet some of Bowthorpe's entrepreneurs and got a head massage from the mobile beauty therapist. People's attitude does seem to have changed in Bowthorpe. I keep meeting people who are talking about starting a business. It is seen as more achievable, a real option for people – whoever they are. And I have come a long way from my initial sessions where I swamped clients with information.

Trust makes all that possible. I have learned, in this short period working as a BizFizz coach, just how crucial this ingredient is if you want something to happen. If you have some measure of trust between you and your managers, and if you can build mutual trust with the client, then really anything is possible. If that trust is missing, in any of these dimensions, then – no matter what the weight of official resources you bring to bear – almost nothing is possible, no matter how brilliant the advisor or the client.

That seems like a simple truth, yet so much of the regeneration business fails to recognise its fundamental importance. Without that trust, the real business of business advice becomes a mirror image of itself. We believe the rhetoric that the clients need the agencies, but in practice, the big agencies need their clients as a reason for their existence. The bigger the agency, the harder it is for them to transform the way they organise themselves, to do away with the nightmare hoops and the petty bureaucracy; the harder it is for them to see clients for what they are, rather than fitting them into pigeon-holes.

And don't under-estimate the impact of this. I had one client who told me about his business idea, having had some experience of regeneration agencies. "I suppose you want me to say when I will be employing people," he said to me sadly. When I told him that was really up to him, he broke down. He was another victim of the way big agencies train their clients in agency-think, when life bears little resemblance to that.

Of course, it is easier to let clients go at their own pace of change, when you are smaller. It is easier to trust them and for them to build a human relationship with you. It is easier for you to understand how destructive it is to demand meetings at set times when your client is in their workshop or picking their child up from school. But I do not believe it is idealistic to expect agencies charged with regeneration to realise that their communities are full of capable, resourceful people, and that what I call 'institutionalised inertia' is dangerously corrosive of goodwill, resources and time. This absolutely central need for trust means that there is really no alternative in the process of releasing the potential in a neighbourhood to genuinely getting involved.

Interlude: A day in the life of a BizFizz coach

"The day starts with great news. The Prince's Trust has agreed to lend a client, Lee, money for his DJ/event promotion business. We talk through what he needs to do next.

Some research: on tree surgery, Permitted Hours of Work for people on incapacity benefit, Access to Work grants, manuscript reading services, setting up a shop on Ebay. I print off an article on structuring sales literature to draw customers to your product for one client, and email it to another.

I return a call to an after-school club, with details of clients who could provide workshops – an environmental artist, a yoga instructor and the Worm Hotel. I head off to meet Ian at Mid-Cheshire College. He is passionate about film-making and music composition, and we consider his options.

While there, I bump into another client, Jane, a children's author, with a friend who is a watercolour painter. They tell me about a new idea combining their talents. It is brilliant. We will meet up next week to talk things through.

After lunch, I catch up with Justin, who wants to set up a tree surgery business. He has almost finished his qualifications and has experience. We work on his business plan so he can apply for funding. He talks through his hopes and fears, and decides what actions to take to investigate the market, insurance and the costs of starting up and running his business. I agree to fix up an appointment with the Welfare Rights Officer at the Citizen's Advice Bureau.

I meet Emma, who runs a successful jewellery business, and is taking time out for some strategic thinking. I have taken her questions to the BizFizz panel and we explore the options with lots of 'what ifs'. She decides to speak to a panel member who has market knowledge and relevant contacts.

I call Paul at the Works – a local charity – to refer a client who may need funding to assist with training, and pick his brains about another client whose idea relates to apprenticeships.

At 4.30, I confirm the arrangements for a workshop which I am planning with the Women's Development Group at the Small Oaks family centre. The conversation sparks more ideas so I go and get a cup of tea in the town centre and sketch out a plan, before heading home."

Victoria Evans,
Winsford, Cheshire

Chapter 3
Passion

Victoria Evans

*"You get the best effort from others not by lighting a fire
beneath them, but by building a fire within."*

Bob Nelson

*"There was just something in my head that wouldn't go away. If
we never try, how are we going to find out if it's going to work?"*
Terry Quinn, BizFizz client, Horden & Easington.

"Mind the gorilla's head!" I stumble slightly and come face to face with
a huge white head.

"I mainly work in bronze but I taught myself to sculpt in stone a few
years ago."

I take a closer look. The gorilla's head is beautifully carved. Its big
empty eyes stare straight at me. We continue the tour of Keith's
garage. He shows me his workbench and he explains how he has
experimented with different designs. He talks me through the 'loss
wax' process for producing bronzes, pointing to pieces of work in various stages. He tells me how he has researched and experimented for
30 years. He shows me an exquisite bronze orangutan and his partial-
ly finished humpback whale breaching out of the water. This is excep-
tionally beautiful work.

Keith is a giant of a man. He grins and says that he has "driven his
family mad" for years with his hobby. Now, after years reading gas
meters, his health has stopped him working like that and he wants to
turn this passion into a business.

I ask what this would mean for him and he doesn't hesitate. It is about
having a livelihood by doing something he loves, about having his
work appreciated by a wider group of people and, more than anything,
it is about meaning. It means leaving some kind of legacy. "Isn't that
what everybody wants?" he asks.

Keith isn't alone. Working as a BizFizz coach in a small town in Cheshire, I have had the privilege of working with people with some amazing passions. Jo wants to create environmental art workshops for children. Tim is proud of his ability to perform electrical testing and re-wire houses. Sue finds great satisfaction in providing a high quality dry-cleaning service. Philip wants to create events for other hard-core dance-music devotees like himself. Justin has wanted to work with trees since he was fourteen. What they have in common and what distinguishes these people from others who might also carry out these activities is the quality of their experience.

I have come to understand from my BizFizz clients that a passion is something that you enjoy for its own sake. You care about it deeply. You find it absorbing. You may lose track of time when you are doing it. A passion is joyful and exciting and somehow makes the world seem right when you are about it. It brings a sense of meaning and purpose. It also brings an opportunity – perhaps your best opportunity – to express who you are and to make your contribution to the world.

Like a fingerprint, your passion is something unique to you. As I have started to explore below the surface of this phenomenon in business coaching, I have discovered that no two people have identical passions. Even in one person's life, a passion may keep showing up in different ways and combinations: it is something that can develop and change over time.

But is Keith right? Does everyone have these desires? Or because we work with people who have a passion, does BizFizz only work with the special few in a community?

It is a Friday morning in the Family Centre in Winsford in Cheshire, where I work. There are about a dozen women – some young and some older – chatting around the room. I have been invited to talk to a women's group which meets regularly and have decided to run a short session on 'Living your Passion'.

I am also feeling a little nervous. I have no idea how this will be received. There is a large plate of cream cakes on the table. I think: if all else fails, at least we can enjoy the cream cakes. I start by sharing what I have noticed about passion while I have been working with

47

BizFizz clients in their town and there is an instant recognition of the idea around the table. What is more, the women immediately start chipping in with their own talents, interests and desires. Within minutes the room is full of passions – a desire to teach mathematics to adults, to sing, to write poetry, to care for animals, an interest in politics.

It confirms what I have come to believe. That passion is a truly empowering concept and that it helps people to find their own power within themselves.[1] But most of all, that passion is a very common human experience. As a coach, I ask "what do you desire?" "What is it about this idea that excites you?" and "What does this mean for you?" all the time, often in places where these questions are not usually asked. But sometimes I hardly need to ask the questions because I am literally tripping over the answers.

The truth is that you find sparks of passion everywhere you find human beings. People simply vary in the role they allow their passions to play in their lives at any particular time. It is a choice to build a fire. The spark for the fire is the desire: "I'd love to….", "I've always wanted to…." The big question is: how does someone take that spark and build the fire? And how does a BizFizz coach support that choice?

––––––––––––

Just as fires need oxygen, passions need dreams. Many people censor their dreams almost as soon as they think about them. They are easily discarded as wishful thinking. As a coach, I encourage people to talk about their big dream.

"What would you love to do if you could do anything?"

I ask them to imagine what it would be like if their dream was a reality. There is often a temptation to stick with small, manageable dreams, so I might ask them to go even further: "What is the biggest version of your passion that you can imagine right now?"

It takes courage to explore the cherished ambitions at the outer edge of a dream, but the gains are often huge if someone is prepared to

––––––––––––

1   I am indebted to the CoachU course on "Empowering Methods" for this definition of empowerment.

take the risk. First, it is more effective in the long run if you get to what you really, really want: a compromise is rarely exciting enough to stimulate you to do what is necessary to get it. You may find yourself stalling with the project later and need to come back to what you really want.

Second, your imagination is an amazing resource. Dreams carry useful messages about what you can do and the directions you can choose. People are often shocked that so many ideas are already there in their heads.

Third, the gap between what you think you can do now and your dream is a creative space.

Take Ian, for example. He had recently started his business. We were looking back over a remarkable year in which he made a massive shift in what he thought he could achieve in his life. He described how expanding his dreams had allowed him to stop feeling 'caged in'. "It's opened up a space in my head," he said. "A fertile space where things can happen."

But what about the risk of failure? Isn't it unfair to raise someone's hopes in this way?

The answer to the question lies in how a coach works with their client. I work with people who I regard as creative, resourceful and whole – which is a key principle of coaching, as defined by the International Coach Federation – no matter what their current circumstances are or what their own assessment of themselves is. This means that I am clear that they are making choices and they can face the question of possible failure as creative human beings.

So I have learnt that my question should not be: "What will happen if you don't succeed?" Instead I ask: "What are you willing to take on that is worth failing at?"

This is a very powerful way to capture the essence of what you want to do. Jane, a children's author, has found it helpful to write out her personal 'statement of intent'. Trevor, a digital art photographer, collects images that remind him of his dream. It is important to have a way to hold your vision, to keep you on track and inspired when everything else threatens to get in the way.

One of my roles as coach is to keep referring back to the original dream as we go along and to ask from time to time: "Is this still on track for you?"

If big dreams are the oxygen for the fire, then there is a very easy way to smother a passion.

Tom is at a very early stage in exploring his ideas for a business. He has investigated one way of moving forward, but this has not really matched what he wants. He shares his ideas with a neighbour who says: "Dreams are OK, but it's turning them into reality that really counts. You have to be practical and live in the real world after all."

That makes him feel stupid that he is unable to provide detailed answers to all the practical points. He is almost ready to give up the whole thing. I have noticed that often the comments from others that really sting us are the ones that echo voices in our own heads telling us what we 'should' be doing. Tom feels he 'should' have all the answers by now. He doubts whether he 'should' be a dreamer at all.

I ask him: "If you gave yourself permission to explore your ideas for a while, what would you do?"

He starts to think of other possibilities which he has barely investigated yet and identifies his next step. I share the thought that questions of profitability and practicality can be wet blankets when they are asked too soon. I suggest that there will come a time in the process when these questions will be appropriate and I am confident that he will tackle them when that time comes.

"I really want to illustrate children's books, but I don't know anything about it and I don't know anyone who does. Perhaps I'd better think of something else...."

It is our first meeting and a lack of knowledge is making Stephanie's dream seem impossible. How can she even begin?

"I've worked with lots of people who didn't know how to move forward with their passions at the beginning," I tell her. "It's a just part of the process. I think you will find the information you need when you need it."

The truth is that, if dreams are the oxygen, then information is often the kindling to help get the fire started. So we get to work. We start by listing what Stephanie already knows about children's book illustration and the publishing industry. This list is longer than she expected. Then I ask her to tell me all the questions she has in her mind at the moment. We make another list. Finally I ask: "What can you do in the next two weeks to find the answers?"

Armed with the specific questions, Stephanie starts to develop some strategies using the internet and the local library. I also offer to send a request for answers to the local panel. I know that one panel member has previous experience in children's book publishing. I notice that a number of Stephanie's questions express a concern that she might not be able to pursue her dream while also caring for her children. Will she have to go to college? Can she work flexibly from home? She is afraid that, having dared to dream, she will get the answers she would prefer not to hear.

Sometimes it takes courage to give up not knowing the answers. But I have another question. "What would it be like if you went through life never knowing whether you could do this?"

When we next meet, Stephanie has assembled an amazing array of information and useful contacts. Even more encouraging, they have all confirmed that she can pursue her dream in the way she had hoped.

Information is important, but building a fire with kindling alone is really not possible. The fire will only really start to build if you introduce more substantial fuel at the same time. There are two good fuels for a passion: action and learning. The strongest fires use both together.

The time to act on your passion is always sooner than you think. It is tempting to put it off: "I'll do it when …." The more important and ambitious the dream, the more tempting this can become. Action is the best antidote to fear. The priority is to develop momentum as soon as possible. You are in a much stronger position to deal with other difficult circumstances in your life if you are already moving forward with your passion.

So in the very first meeting, I find myself asking: "What can you do to take this forward now?"

The first step can be small and simple to accomplish. It is just important to begin. Beginning means signalling to yourself that you are serious. It is like putting a marker down, a statement of intent.

Taking action is enormously satisfying. It builds your confidence. It moves you away from identifying with poverty and lack. When you identify what you can do right now, you start to appreciate the resources you already have. I often encourage clients to make two lists: the resources they already have to support their passion and the resources they have yet to find. The first list is almost always longer than people expect. As for the second list, it is always helpful to work on the assumption that you will find these resources when you need them.

"How can you start doing what you want to do right now?"

Rachel has just opened her own catering business in her new premises, but she started by organising the catering for a number of large family parties. By doing this, she learned how to estimate quantities, the costs involved, the kinds of items which were popular and which were not, the logistics of food production and delivery. She also learnt what she enjoys doing and what she hates doing. It meant that she could decide what kind of catering business she wanted and could plan in detail how to set it up.

Action gives you more information to work with. It is always worth exploring whether you can create some kind of 'dress rehearsal' so that you can experiment with your ideas.

"Whatever you can do, or dream, begin it now," goes a quotation attributed, among others, to Goethe. "Boldness has genius, power and magic in it."

Richard set up his own drama school and he has this quotation on his website. It has a special meaning for him. When he advertised his first drama class, he received only six serious enquiries. He wanted twenty or more. What to do? He decided to start with six students.

"If we had waited to fill the class, we would never have started," he says now. "Starting created a momentum and others started to come along. The class is now full and I've just started a second class of students."

Learning provides greater freedom to act: it is liberating when you see the actions you take as opportunities to learn. Setting aside notions of success and failure, I ask: "What does this tell you? What have you learned?" Seeing failure as information feedback allows you to keep moving. You make better decisions as you learn.

The process of learning also draws out your natural resilience. It is often a profound shift from failure to feedback: some BizFizz clients are acutely aware that they have been judged to have failed because they didn't do well at school or because they are living on benefits.

That mistake at least has to be overcome. "Everyone is born a genius," wrote the artist, architect and futurist Buckminster Fuller, "but the process of living de-geniuses them." As you build your passion, your fire within, you learn to appreciate your own genius.

You may feel uncomfortable with this idea at first. A genius, after all, is a rare and special person. Yet, when I work with someone as they build their passion, I start to see their unique gifts. These gifts often hide in notions of common sense. I have come to the conclusion that everybody has a different definition of common sense because everybody has different gifts which are so natural to them that they assume everyone else must have them, too.

Actually, not everyone can develop a supportive network for their ideas without even thinking about it, but to Rachel it is 'common sense'. Not everyone can devise at least a dozen alternative strategies while making a cup of tea, but for Lee that is normal. Not everyone can thrive in the uncertainty of the development phase of a project, but to Maggie this is her natural environment and she is bored anywhere else.

Quite often, the individual has been criticised rather than affirmed for their gifts. They may have picked up labels – a butterfly, dreamer or pushy – so they may limit or hide their use. In the context of their passion, these gifts become their strongest resources. As a coach, it is my job to celebrate them and to encourage their use. A passion – the desire to venture upon something new – comes because you are ready to grow and to achieve more of your potential. It is an opportunity to express more of your genius.

At the deepest level, following your passion is about learning to trust yourself. You learn to trust that your desire to do something is worth pursuing. You learn to trust that you have the strengths and abilities to match your passion. You learn that you can trust your own ability to make powerful choices.

"So basically I've screwed it up."

Graham looks dejected. He has just explained that, after a year of running his business, he has "got himself into a financial mess". He has underestimated the seasonal effects in his market and his debts are mounting. He feels that he is what he calls a "complete failure".

I listen and notice that this young man is very precise about what he has done and what he could have done. He impresses me as someone who thinks clearly and takes decisions. I tell him: "I think you are someone who has the strength to make the right decisions when they are needed."

He looks up, puzzled. Then, when he has decided that I'm serious, he starts to tell me some of the ideas he has had to turn his financial situation around. Over the next few months, he implements a range of strategies and most of them work. Six months later, he is back on a sound financial footing.

I find that people always know what to do, although they may be out of the habit of trusting themselves. This 'knowing' takes different forms for different people. One client refers to his 'wise plan', another talks about a quiet voice in her head. Yet another checks her 'gut feelings'.

My own journey as a BizFizz coach has involved learning to trust my own intuition and encouraging my clients to trust theirs. I often think this is a muscle people are aware of but are just not using enough yet.

It does take effort to start a fire. It needs time and attention to keep it going. But pursuing your passion need not be a struggle. One of the reasons why BizFizz works with passion is because a passion creates its own natural motivation. In fact, your motivation levels can provide a useful guidance system. You know you are on track with the right passion because you feel alive, happy and fulfilled. Doing work you don't like takes more effort and is often more costly in the long run. Other people may perceive that you are making sacrifices for your passion, but the point is that it won't feel like that to you.

Like clearing the ground for a fire, I often work with clients as they realise that they need to give up some activities to move forward with their passion but these will always be commitments which they didn't really want in their life anyway. They often feel huge relief when they let them go.

It is important to notice if working on your passion is becoming a struggle. "I really need to get myself motivated about this," said Louise, sinking back into her sofa. She looked distinctly unmotivated. She seemed smaller than she did a few minutes ago when she described her vision for her social enterprise. The enterprise was a passion for her and it was developing well but she said she was getting "bogged down" in administrative tasks. She was trying to force herself to do them.

"If you were going to do this in a way that you could really enjoy, what would you do?" I said.

"I wouldn't do these jobs and I would concentrate on fundraising."

"What would be the impact of that?"

"I would be putting my effort into the most important thing. It's also the thing I really enjoy because I know I can do it well. If I concentrate on it, I could bring in the funding quicker so the organisation would grow."

"What could you do to make that happen?"

"Well, now that I think about it, some of the administration tasks could be left for now... And I know someone who would enjoy doing the other tasks. I'd need to explain what to do but I know she could do it and she wants a bigger role."

Whenever someone is losing their motivation, when they are bored, restless or uninspired, I encourage them to use their feelings as a cue to think differently. It suggests that there is a better way. Is this really your passion or is it someone else's? Does your passion need a new outlet? Are you focusing on the wrong area? Could someone else take a role?

Fiona shows me some tiny sea shells which she has made from icing sugar and painted with edible inks to produce a marbled, translucent effect. They are exquisite. She has started a business based on her passion for designing, making and decorating cakes. Her loving attention to detail extends to every area of her business. She takes care to buy the highest quality ingredients. She is constantly trying new ideas. She is always looking for ways to do extra for her customers. She is already building a reputation for delightful, original cake decoration and her customer base is growing. Her passion means that she is naturally motivated to do what it takes.

Watching her at work, I realise that passion is also a very practical concept, because loving what you do makes success more likely. This is not just hocus pocus, because passion is attractive for the customer, too.

Susan wants to set up a domestic cleaning business. For her, this is a passion. She talks about the pleasure she feels when she creates a clean, beautiful space for others to live in. If you were looking for a cleaning service, wouldn't you rather employ her than someone who seemed to be doing it because they couldn't think of anything better to do?

As a BizFizz coach, I help people to build their own fires within. The concept of passion is powerful. I introduce the word into a conversation and something is released. The conversation always leaps forward with an amazing energy as the other person takes the invitation to talk. I start to glimpse the astonishing qualities of the person I am talking to. I see their uniqueness and I feel privileged.

A passionate client has a big enough agenda for the both of us. I don't need to invent one for them. Instead, my job is to support them to dream the biggest dreams, to gather the information and resources they need, and to find within themselves the courage to take action and learn to trust themselves and their passion.

When we work with someone's passions in regeneration, everyone's relationship with struggling shifts. For the individual client, their passion can be bigger than their struggles and allow them to deal with other aspects of their life from a position of personal power. For someone working to achieve regeneration within a community, leveraging passion demands that any burden of struggling to fix people and situations has to go. It means allowing people to set their own big agenda and trusting in their ability and energy to take it forward.

Interlude: Sweet Earth, Leicester

"I've always been interested in business; I knew that I wanted to do my own stuff. Now I'm running an online supermarket offering organic products. I did some research, and I talked to Business Link. But they aren't talking face to face to people any more. After that, I decided to do it all myself.

I wrote my business plan, went round to talk to banks, shopped around for premises. Then I met Natalia (BizFizz coach). She has helped with a lot of things, particularly contacts and advice. Now I'll take her advice before doing anything.

Running a business feels great, but it's hard work. You shouldn't go into it for the money – that comes much later. It's the thrill and motivation – you need to have passion, faith and fire. You've got to have faith in yourself – and if you don't trust yourself then you won't be able to get anywhere."

Vimal Morjaria

Chapter 4
Client focused

Paul Davies

"Grown-ups love figures. When you tell them that you've made a new friend, they never ask you any questions about essential matters. They never say to you 'What does his voice sound like? What games does he love best? Does he collect butterflies?' Instead they demand 'How old is he? How much does he weigh? How much money does his father make?' Only from these figures do they think they have learned anything about him."

Antoine de Saint-Exupery, The Little Prince

"The BizFizz model is about helping communities feel better about themselves. Numerical analysis doesn't show the effect of role models appearing in communities or an increasing 'can do' attitude."

Gary Cliffe, Winsford BizFizz
Local Management Group member

It was a terrible night when we met for one particular BizFizz panel meeting. It was freezing cold and the rain was pouring down. There was a noisy gale blowing outside as I waited in the school staff room in Clowne, which we were using for that month's panel meeting, for the members to turn up. On a night like that, it seemed unlikely that many would arrive, but I was wrong.

One by one, the panel regulars – local business people, council officials, the local headmaster, someone from the Inland Revenue, someone from Business Link – emerged from the storm, dripping wet and windblown, their anoraks making small puddles on the floor. To my surprise, the turn-out was excellent, and by the time the meeting was due to begin, the small staff room was packed. We managed to squeeze in, and could hear the rain pounding outside the windows which threatened to drown out the conversation.

In fact, that evening, we only had one client case to discuss. It was a woman who wanted to set up a beauty and alternative therapy practice in a building that she was buying. The question put to the panel was how to develop her marketing strategy. By the end of the evening, we had pages and pages of flip chart paper covered in ideas, names and phone numbers that the client could follow up. Fifteen heads had been put together focusing on this client's business, and together we had been able to produce a marketing plan that was rooted in real, local, personal contacts. "Do you know," one of the panel said to me at the end of the meeting, "I felt this woman's life actually changing in front of me."

The independence of the panel members, and the networks and enthusiasm they bring to the table every time they meet, is discussed in other chapters. What I want to emphasise here is the power to find solutions when all these minds focus on the business issues of one individual. It was her success they were concentrating on – not how she could help them reach their own funders' targets, serve official agendas, or bring direct benefit to themselves – and her success as *she* saw it developing, success on the client's terms.

There are people on the BizFizz panel in Clowne, which is in Derbyshire, who have worked in regeneration for many years. They are rightly proud of what they have achieved over the years, but they also talk occasionally about failings within the regeneration industry, with its years of frustration, and its money spent on unsuccessful, top-down initiatives. They have seen capital programmes that left a legacy of new buildings and facilities but still no reductions in underlying deprivation. They have seen the role of individual entrepreneurs as drivers for regeneration ignored and sidelined.

But they also recognise that BizFizz works. "BizFizz is doing what it should do," they say. "Things happen – people come here to do stuff." I know they value seeing the businesses start up, because they tell me so. They also like being involved first hand in helping people to move forward and achieve what they want. And what makes this exciting, paradoxically, is that it is not numbers and targets that are driving the process – it is their concern for the needs of these individual clients. It is this human element at the core of the BizFizz approach that distinguishes it.

When I arrived as the coach in Clowne, I quickly realised that the local perception of the place was as an economic victim. I was often told that Clowne was an ex-mining community that had "the heart sucked out of it". Equally, I was told by some people who lived there that Clowne was a place where people just wanted to buy things cheap. About the last thing it seemed to them to be was an entrepreneurial place.

I learned to doubt this perception by meeting other people in the town, and I soon realised that the impression was seriously out of date. The last pit actually closed two decades ago. In just over a year and a half, in which BizFizz has been running in Clowne, there has been a difference in local businesses that people like Tony, a local businessman and chair of my local management group, tells me is quite noticeable. Specialist shops have opened: Serenity health and beauty centre, an interior design shop, a ladies clothing store, a florist.

In a town which was popularly supposed to have had "the heart sucked out of it", the diversity of BizFizz clients was really astonishing. We have seen child minders and handymen, of course, but we have also seen an industrial artist, a milkman, a psychic, a graffiti artist, a worm farmer, a motor cycle training school, a poet and many others. These are not people that BizFizz has somehow created. They were in Clowne already, and I think some of those who wrote the town off have been amazed at the entrepreneurial talent and creative energy that has emerged here. I believe their involvement with BizFizz has helped many of these entrepreneurs get into business and make things happen. And the thing which has made the real difference here has been that we have been able to focus on them as individuals – on their ideas in their own right – and have not been following some official business support blueprint that had been decided in Whitehall.

There is an inevitable question about the sustainability of this kind of individual attention, and we should address it. Doesn't the coach get overloaded?

The answer is that this is a juggling act. It is a question of managing the time with each client so that I can be flexible to meet their needs. I have never been in a position where I can't see a client for more than a few days. In 21 months, I have seen 130 clients, and it is true that this is much less than a mainstream business advisor who has clients block booked every hour, every day. But the remit of mainstream business advisors is to service a much wider geographical region than a BizFizz coach. The population of my patch is approximately 8,000.

One accusation that was put to BizFizz in the run-up to funding the second phase is that, because BizFizz programmes only target a small geographical area, they cannot be considered 'strategic'. There seems to be a belief among the various national and regional bodies that, unless something is capable of pan-galactic application, it is not worth doing. I would argue otherwise. To me, 'strategic' means providing appropriate solutions in appropriate places. The broad-brush approach favoured by some funders and regional development agencies is not actually strategic at all. It is simply a blanket. Of course, it may be a great deal easier to manage a business support product centrally, where you can define the options available to clients and predict the take-up of activities without reference to different realities on the ground. Many support programmes are based on data – or just assumptions – showing what issues small business start-ups have often asked for help with: sales, marketing or websites for example. This is then converted into standardised training courses or support programmes that are thrust at everyone, no matter what their needs. That is 'strategic' they say, and therefore – theoretically, at least – it is cost-effective.

But this conventional business support is based on average solutions. Out of my 130 clients, a small minority have made effective use of the standard training courses, and other generic help packages available. Standardised support programmes might be the most cost-effective way to churn out 'pile-it-high-sell-it-cheap' business support, but in practice it is not clear how many people really benefit, where are these standard entrepreneurs which are supposed to fit these 'one-size fits all' standard approaches to support?

The American business writer Gerald Weinberg has a principle that he calls the 'Raspberry Jam Law'. It states that the further you spread your service, the thinner it gets, until it eventually has very little impact at all. "Slather a bit of raspberry jam on a few slices of bread, and you'll see each stroke get thinner and thinner," he writes in his book *More Secrets of Consulting*. You have to make a choice, he says, between distribution and depth. Between numbers of people being touched by the service on offer, and the actual benefit that each individual derives from that service.

Big institutions spreading systematic programmes of business support and advice over large areas should not be surprised if they fall victim to the Raspberry Jam Law. But there are some types of jam that have lumps, to continue the metaphor, and which stop them from being spread too thinly. For BizFizz, the lumps of fruit are the basic relationships between the entrepreneur, the coach and the panel. Client-focused support is based on this relationship. If that is your purpose in business advice, then it will not get spread too thinly. The limit of spread is the capacity of the coaches and their networks.

Only by completely focusing on the client can you hope to uncover the hidden issues that clients face when setting up their business, and support the client to deal with them. The example in the first chapter of the client who had been persuaded by the Job Centre to set up a decorating business when he actually wanted to be a hang-gliding teacher could not happen in BizFizz. Yes, that limits the reach of BizFizz: we never try to process a certain number of clients through the door in any given day. Yes, that means that BizFizz is not amenable to pan-galactic application with virtual, or remote, delivery. But then we are in the business of supporting clients from within the community to start their business on their own terms. That is what makes BizFizz effective in communities where mainstream agencies have failed to find entrepreneurs to support to start with, and then written those communities off as having no entrepreneurs. Our experience challenges this assumption, and challenges support agencies to become client focused in their delivery.

So you want to be your own boss. You have a business idea, a dream, and you are absolutely passionate about it. Your product or service will be different or more accessible or better value than others can provide. But where do you start? It is likely to be new territory for you. It is probably a bit scary and you could do with some help. What support would really help you turn your business idea into a reality?

Would it satisfy you, for example, to be given a list of training courses and programmes and asked which ones you would like to go on first? Or to be given a template for a business plan and invited to go away and fill it out before you go any further? Or maybe to be given a copy of *21 Easy Steps to Launching your Business* along with some pro forma marketing materials? Or would you really prefer to be asked what help you actually need and then given focused support to meet those individual needs?

Some of us might say that any of the above could be useful ways to help people gain a bit of insight and understanding into what business is about. But I think the rest of us would shrug and say that we should work out exactly what any individual client needs before setting out on any course of action. The trouble is that, in practice, most of what is available to start up a new business in this country falls into the first few categories above. Often it is increasingly the limit. Mainstream business support services are moving towards what they call 'universal start-up programmes' which have much less emphasis on face-to-face, client-focused support. Output targets and centrally driven objectives are in danger of taking precedence over the widely varied requirements of individual entrepreneurs.

The growth of managerial targets in the public sector has been one of the main changes over the past decade. The idea of reducing the component parts of what an institution is supposed to be achieving and measuring them dates back to the time-and-motion ideas of Frederick Winslow Taylor. It has been given new life more recently with the growth of large quangos that governments have set up to deliver services, and which they then feel the need to control. Targets allow central bureaucrats to have control over the details of what frontline professionals are doing. Or at least to have the illusion of control. Goodhart's Law, formulated by a former director of the Bank of England, explains that output measures, when used as methods of control, will always be inaccurate. Staff always find ways of working the numbers rather than working to achieve what really needs to be done. Often that results in behaviour and action that is completely contrary to what had been intended.

This is partly the result of fearful central bureaucracies under political pressure. Their intentions seem superficially quite reasonable – to make sure, for example, that business support covers the full spectrum of gender and race. But in practice, on the ground, the plethora of generic targets that business support has to fulfil – on the number of business start-ups, number of jobs created or the ethnicity or gender of a client – are superficial, end up skewing how business support is provided in an area, and cloud what should be the real objectives of supporting enterprise in communities in the first place. That is, supporting individuals to achieve their business dreams. Helping those that want to be helped, not just those that you want to help.

A target-driven culture means that administrative systems are in danger of dominating mainstream business support delivery to the extent that clients become processed rather than helped. It can become hard to allow them the space and time to express their passions for the businesses they wish to develop. These processes take the 'people' out of business. They give an illusion of simplicity. They also provide some bizarre examples of Goodhart's Law in practice. "If a man and a woman come in together," we have heard it suggested, "put them both down as female – we're short of those."

These target systems fail to support entrepreneurs, but they also serve to restrict the freedom of advisors to do their job. Many business advisors are dedicated and have a passion for what they do. The responsibility of the business support agency is to harness this dedication, but often in practice they burden them with systems that result in the processing of clients.

If your funder sets a target of 50 new business start-ups, the business advisor will have to keep one eye on the funder's needs when working with a client. When faced with a client who is just not ready to start their business, what sort of perverse pressure is that putting on the advisor? They have the choice – do the right thing for the client but miss your targets, or meet your targets by encouraging the client to invest time and money in a business that will almost certainly fail. Hardly best practice, is it? In the short term, it may result in increased numbers of business start-ups. But will this just be achieved at the expense of the sustainability of these new ventures. The point is that *how* support is provided is fundamental to the long-term success of that business.

In Clowne, BizFizz has received excellent support and co-operation from our local Business Link, and that partnership has worked both ways. A Business Link advisor is on my local management group, and is a member of the local panel. I have referred clients to them when they have had certain training or research needs. They have managed to find grant funding for some clients. Business Link has also referred people on to me if they have been based in Clowne and if they might benefit from the closer one-to-one coaching they will get via BizFizz.

But they are under pressure. As Business Links bid for the rights to deliver the 'Universal Start-up Offering' from March 2007 onwards, they are finding it harder to provide the personal, one-to-one support that they know is of most benefit to the individuals.

One client came to me with a plan for a mobile cleaning business. We had found finance to get the equipment he needed and he was ready to start, but he still needed help selling his service in the local area. Now, the traditional approach here might have been to suggest that he get himself booked onto a two-day marketing and sales training course to improve his core skills. This might have given him the principles of selling, but probably would not have brought him new business in a practical way.

Instead, we used our sessions to look at the best areas to start selling locally and I put him in touch with someone who would distribute his leaflets so he could get cracking straight away. I put the question to the local BizFizz panel, and they came up with the names and contacts of local car dealers who could use his service. They also suggested that the client went round the pubs and clubs and offered to clean their carpets and upholstery. This turned out to be a real money spinner – and it was something the client would probably not have thought of himself. These were very local, very personal and very specific contacts and ideas. They are not available from training courses.

These contacts have now given the client a great deal more confidence. When he first came to see me, he was on benefits and quite cautious. His wife was nervous about the idea of him starting up a business. It felt like a big risk. They have a disabled daughter but managed to find financial stability through the benefit payments they received. But the client hated this feeling of dependence. It undermined his self-esteem and sapped his confidence.

I met him and his wife a couple of times and helped them weigh up the comparative risks and opportunities. His wife came around to supporting the business idea and this was very important. Now, the client is bullish. He has gone out, followed up these contacts, and is bringing in enough trade to sustain a successful business. What he needed to be able do this was help that was tailored to his needs, not an uneasy fit between his needs and whatever happened to be available off-the-shelf with standard approaches.

On the other hand, client focus does not mean a kind of capitulation to an unrealistic client's agenda. Business has a hard reality and the client-focused support has to explore this. You have to bring your own experience as a coach to bear on the relationship but, in exploring the reality, it is the client that has to make the decisions about what they are prepared to do – as coach you support this process.

My background includes setting up a consultancy business with partners. I started working from my spare room and then, together with the partners, we grew it into a business with a turnover of £4 million. This experience of abandoning my job and regular salary, suddenly not having those cheques appearing every month, and having to build up the business, means that I know what it feels like to have to do everything yourself. I would find myself photocopying at 2am on a Monday morning to prepare manuals for a workshop I was running later that day. At the beginning, everything sits on your shoulders and the main priority is selling. Later on, when the business grew bigger, we still made sure that all our staff, whenever they visited clients, were aware that they needed to try and sell in the next piece of business. That remains the bottom line.

Some BizFizz clients come to see me with very romantic ideas of what they would like to do. There have been a few people wanting to set up shops locally. In these cases, we looked at what exactly was involved in developing the ideas and running the business. With one client we did a quick profit and loss projection and she soon realised that this was simply not a viable business proposition.

I took another client to a shop in Chesterfield that sold similar stock to the one he wanted to open in Clowne. We stood there, looking at the value of stock in the shop, and counting the number of customers that came in. When we got back, he realised that he would never be able to get that kind of footfall in Clowne. It was just an unrealistic proposition. Another client was producing garden ornaments and I felt he was seriously under-pricing them. We went mystery shopping at a couple of other garden centres to see how other people were pricing similar products. As a result, he began selling his work for around three times the price.

This involves working with clients to be realistic. But again, it is hands on. And it is quite different from sending people off with a template business plan and telling them to go away and fill it in. Often these pro-forma templates ask all about the idea, the product lines, the legal aspects and the marketing, but ignore the financial underpinnings of the business until right at the end. In reality, the sales targets and finances are where many people need to start – job number 1. It is one thing to produce a glossy business plan on paper, but quite another to face the reality of who exactly you think your first customers will be, how much they will pay and whether you will attract enough of them to sustain a profitable business.

Then there are the other clients, quite often tradespeople, who are trained and have well-formed and viable business ideas. What many of them feel they lack is a better understanding of how to sell themselves. They come looking for sales support aids. But actually, this is not usually what they really need – many people underestimate how good they are at selling. If they know what they are doing, and can talk with passion and understand their customer's needs, then they probably already have what they think they need.

One client said he "didn't do selling" and asked me to come to a meeting with one of his customers. I really had to do nothing because, once his customer explained what he was looking for, my client instantly understood his needs and got busy explaining how he could help, doing drawings to show what he meant and responding to questions. They had a lively conversation about how my client could help provide exactly what was needed.

Towards the end of the meeting, the customer asked how much it would cost and I noticed my client started to jot down a few figures. I interrupted and suggested that he send through a quote tomorrow. Afterwards, my client started to run through how much it would cost him and then just added on 20 per cent to the costs as his mark-up. I explained that this customer was a definite buyer and that price probably wasn't an important factor. He agreed in the end that instead of charging 50p per unit, he could charge £1.40 per unit. The buyer accepted.

Many clients have difficulty and embarrassment over pricing and valuing their products and services. One business I worked with produced a beautiful stationery product and had customers falling over themselves to buy them. They wanted to expand but they said they just could not afford to move to larger premises or take on staff. I asked them, where they saw themselves in terms of quality.

67

"Well, we're the best," they said.

"Where do you see yourself in terms of price?" I asked.

"We're the cheapest."

When I asked them why this was, they said that – since they were new to the market – they felt they could not charge as much as their more established competitors. In fact, of course, customers have no idea whether a business is new or not and, in any case, there is no reason why this should affect the price they are prepared to pay. That client agreed to increase their prices by 40 per cent and business is still booming. This will make a huge difference to their bottom line and to the growth of their business.

Client focus also means that I can end up doing very practical work to support clients. One person was trying to secure a grant to refurbish their shop front, but they were too busy to organise for builders to come around and give quotes. So I did this and showed the builders around the shop while my client was out with customers. I also drove around with the grant form to get the various signatures required and delivered the application form in time. This only took about 60 minutes in total, but it removed a vital barrier and meant that my client got the grant they needed.

Not the job of a business coach you might say? But in each of the above cases, that small piece of practical help made a fundamental difference to that entrepreneur's future. You might also say that it was not a valuable use of the coach's time. But then, try telling that to the entrepreneurs who benefited.

A couple of clients have asked for help with negotiations with landlords. In one case, by acting as an independent mediator, a client got four initial weeks rent-free. In another, a landlord has agreed to pay for building improvements.

But often client focus means helping to discover the story behind the story. I have one client who popped into see me two or three times a week for fifteen-minute chats. This went on for weeks. He had set up a business that provides a useful service and it looked viable. But he was constantly coming in with new ideas and never seemed to want to focus on putting the time into building his core business. After a while, he confided that he had large debts and was being chased for the money. The bailiffs were looming. This was, in fact, the real issue: he needed to make some quick money. That is why he felt he didn't have the time to focus on the main business.

I got some help from one of the other BizFizz coaches who had a lot of experience in this area. He gave some excellent advice and we started contacting each debtor to make offers and start a discussion. I have acted as an intermediary and a couple of them have reduced the debt they are expecting. This in turn has eased the pressure, and allowed the client to spend more time concentrating on his business rather than flitting from one idea to the next. He is not out of the woods yet, but hopefully he is on his way.

There is another issue about client focus, and that is the question of dependency. Is there not a danger that my clients will become dependent on me?

Possibly there is. That means that a coach needs to be trained to avoid that risk and recognise the difference between crucial intervention and abrogation of responsibility by the entrepreneur. Coaches know how to say no when clients show signs of becoming too dependent, or when they just seem to be enjoying the friendship or social interaction. That is an important part of the training process for business coaching. But there is another feature of BizFizz that reduces this danger. We have developed a system that can create and reinforce temporary teams to support clients.

Few individuals possess all the skills and attributes they need to build a successful business. They may have technical flair related to their chosen profession but may have a complete blank when it comes to financial matters.

"Aha!" says the trainer. "The answer is to get them booked onto courses on basic book-keeping." But not everybody wants to acquire these skills themselves and often there are better ways of closing the financial gap. Friends or family may be able to contribute as the business gets going; local businesses or professionals may be prepared to defer payment of fees or accept services in payment. One client setting up a selling agency has paid for the development of his website by doing some promotional work for the web designers.

Often what clients really need are contacts, especially going to meet other business owners. Some people around here have run businesses for 20 years and have a huge numbers of contacts. Several of these people sit on the BizFizz panel and they are remarkably generous with their time and advice for new entrepreneurs in the area. Another of my clients was looking for some contacts in the garment trade and one of the panel members knew exactly who she should contact – a customer of his who runs an overseas garment manufacturing and importing business in Bolsover, four miles down the road.

"Here," he says. "Tell her to call Bob on this number and say that I suggested she call." These kind of personal contacts are absolutely invaluable.

Other panel members give my clients extended credit terms or help by passing on stock, lending equipment or space. One of my clients was looking for shelving for his workshop but had no time or money to knock some up himself. Dave, a local business owner who sits on the BizFizz panel, said he had got some in his yard up for grabs. When my client came round, his car was too small to fit them in, so Dave chucked him the keys to one of his vans so he could transport the shelves. They had never met each other before, but he felt able to trust and help him in the most practical of ways.

All these relationships take some of the pressure off the coach because there are other people in the community that really want to see new businesses succeed and help out where they can.

My work as a BizFizz coach has given me a fairly clear picture of what the real needs of many aspiring entrepreneurs are. It is also increasingly clear to us in BizFizz that, while the existing regional support programmes provide for some of these needs, there are important gaps which a locally based, community-centred approach has been extremely effective in bridging. The success of the BizFizz approach has been due to its complete flexibility and its absolute focus on the needs of individual entrepreneurs. Those who have received support said that the help they received had made a vital difference. We have seen enough clients now, and heard enough stories, to know that is true.

We had some fantastic news recently. Our local district council, in partnership with two of its neighbours, has recently bid for and been allocated a large sum of money under the government's Local Enterprise Growth Initiative. The great thing about this is that the money will go straight into the deprived areas that have bid for the funding. It will be spent on the real priorities that have been identified in consultation with local people, and it will not be surrounded by heavy-handed target systems which might distort the way in which it is used. It will pay for BizFizz programmes to be set up in additional towns where they would be appropriate, it will pay for specialist advisors to get out and work face-to-face with businesses, and it will address some of the other issues flagged up by small businesses like how they can bid successfully for tenders from large local authorities. We hope there are some promising times ahead for aspiring local entrepreneurs.

So what are the lessons of this? Potential entrepreneurs exist absolutely everywhere. Inspiring and supporting them can make an enormous difference to the places they set up in business. The kind of help they need to do that has to include support that adapts to what they need as individuals, without expecting them to conform to prescribed models, and without setting artificial boundaries to the kind of support they can expect to receive. It also means help with discovering their own potential – and help building their own 'virtual support teams' from within the local and extended business communities.

The BizFizz lesson for business support also means setting free the advisors to be professional and effective. To spread these lessons, we need institutions that can:

- Be responsive to the client's agenda, which means genuinely becoming a learning organisation.

- Use performance management systems with a light touch – without burdening advisors with bureaucracy.

- Be flexible and active in the support of clients, rather than institutionally process-driven.

- Get out into the communities they serve.

- Refrain from taking decisions on behalf of those communities – but ask them instead. Trust begins with transparency.

- Embed the value of client-focused delivery as a core value, and create systems and practice that reflect this value.

There is an assumption that this kind of flexibility can only be possible in small organisations. Yet some very large businesses do manage to be successful simply because they are successful at understanding local needs and adapting to them. Just because institutions are big does not mean they are unable to adapt and allow that kind of individual focus. Yet the public sector seems to find it hard to learn this lesson. Pressure is being applied so that business support is increasingly being developed as blanket coverage. Job Centres also find themselves at the sharp end of constant budget cuts and reappraisals, and find it increasingly difficult to adapt to the specific needs of their clients.

In many ways, BizFizz demonstrates in practice a different approach for the public sector. There is a central set of values, principles and training. It appoints accomplished, resourceful, entrepreneurial people who then adapt the service they are providing to meet the needs of the clients. And they are left to do this without interference.

Practitioners who work face-to-face with entrepreneurs are in broad agreement that there is no real substitute for flexible, practical, personal advice and support for new and growing businesses. Obviously there are cheaper ways of providing nominal services to serve this group, but it is doubtful whether they are effective. Of course, it is possible to handle high numbers of queries by providing telephone support, information websites, proforma business plans and templates for marketing plans and materials, but you have to ask whether this alone has any chance of enriching the local enterprise community.

Interlude: advising or coaching

"I have to thank a client called Simon Bailey – my seventh client – for proving to me that I was a BizFizz coach and not just another business advisor.

Simon had already been dealing with a 'Business Support Agency' for several months which was ostensibly assisting him whilst he set up in business. However, when I met him, he had no defined product or service and had spent the last few months just doing things related to music that would earn him money.

If I am being honest, before BizFizz, I would probably have advised him along similar lines to his existing advisor, which seemed to be based upon 'go out there and earn money doing whatever you can'. To Simon, it felt as if 'it was like herding cats'. However, armed with my recent BizFizz training, we started by both identifying what he had done, and more importantly what he wanted to do.

It soon emerged that his 'passion' was for both music and for education. Simon readily acknowledges that he was not very studious when he was a youth, which he put down largely to not being inspired whilst at school. Now, as a parent, he wanted to ensure that today's youths were given more opportunities to be inspired.

We soon developed an IT-based music course which inspired students to improve a number of key skills, including Numeracy, Literacy, Working With Others, whilst composing and producing their own song/ piece of music. Working together, we then identified potential customers for him, presented together to win business and also to obtain accreditation for the course.

This IT-course has gone down extremely well with groups dealing with disadvantaged youths and his first course inspired one such youth to study harder and win a place on a specialist music course. So not only has BizFizz had a positive impact for Simon, but also for his customers.

Simon's business – Audio Visual Studio – is going from strength to strength and has begun diversifying into other areas – and all because someone talked to him about what <u>he</u> passionately wanted to do, rather than what they thought he should do!"

Peter Waistrell, BizFizz Coach

Chapter 5
Networks

Natalia Fernandez

"Mutual aid is as much a law of animal life as mutual struggle."
Prince Kropotkin

"BizFizz was just what I needed. The coach knew who to get in touch with and put us in for a grant. I didn't know what I needed to do to start a business."
Mick and Sharron Eland, Tuxford

I first met Vimal Mojaria at the Leicester Asian Business Association which, like me, is working to build support for business in the Belgrave Heartlands and the Latimer area of the city. It was very early in the morning and I was the only staff member there.

There is a main street running right through the area which is buzzing with small businesses, from eateries to suppliers of stationery to furniture. The office is at one end and it can seem a little strange because it was originally a bank, and there are two counters with glass panels on one side as you walk in – as if you have come to somewhere to borrow money. Still, Vimal rang the doorbell and I let him in and we barely needed to talk at all before I could see that this was someone who was absolutely passionate about his business idea.

After about 20 minutes, he suddenly handed me a bound business plan, explaining: "This is my business plan, but I don't give it to anybody. You can have it because I trust you."

Vimal left Kenya at the age of 19 and came to Leicester to study accountancy at De Montfort University. He is a strict Hindu, and one of the first things he noticed when he arrived in the UK was the food he was eating. It just didn't taste as good, and he realised that it was manufactured, rarely fresh and had lost much of its flavour. As the years went by, he came to realise that what was needed was a better supply of organic ingredients.

From there, it was a small step to realise there was business potential in supplying this better quality food. If he could taste the difference, then there were probably large numbers of other people who could do so as well, and would pay for an alternative. He was right: his business Sweet Earth was launched in Leicester at the end of 2004 and has now launched in London as well.

Of course it makes good sense – when you have an excellent business idea – to be very careful who you share the details with. But a secret business plan is a problem. To raise the interest necessary to get suppliers and big customers, or to raise the money in the first place, some aspects of it at least are going to have to be shared.

One of the myths about entrepreneurs is that they are rugged individualists, the equivalent of lone gunmen in the Wild West – without friends or supporters – carving out a living in a brutal and unfriendly world. There may be elements of this caricature that are occasionally true: entrepreneurs do need a measure of determination. But it is a cliché that has turned generations of brilliant potential business people off the whole idea. It is also nonsense. To succeed in business, you need – almost above all else – to know people. You need networks of advisors, supporters and friends and you need to be able to understand what they need, too.

So Vimal simply had to be able to share his business plan, not just with me, but with other people who might be able to help and advise him. We went through the plan in more detail and decided that some of the ideas were not within his reach straight away – we replaced the shop with a delivery service – and then we took some of the outstanding issues to the BizFizz panel.

From the very beginning, Vimal had decided that his customers would most likely be people with a high disposable income. I was less sure about this, and the feedback the panel gave also challenged his assumption. As a result, Vimal came to see his potential customers differently. The people with the money might best be able to afford his food, but they might not be the people with the strongest motivation to buy it. He would need to find a way to reach people with strong beliefs around organic food.

This was where the network represented by the panel could be most useful. Actually, of course, Vimal had not kept his business plan secret.

But until he started working with BizFizz, he had asked his most trusted circle of friends for advice. But they tended to think the way he did and did not feel able to challenge his ideas. He was planning to start delivering to homes in London. But at first, advised by his friends, he had dismissed the idea of making deliveries on Sundays. Making deliveries would be easier then, because the traffic would be clearer, but he and his friends thought that the customers would prefer to keep their Sundays free. The feedback from the panel made him change his mind: he does offer deliveries on a Sunday and it has, in fact, proved very popular.

But the panel was useful in other ways too. One of the members owns a marketing company called Bix Promotions. They offered free meetings and are continuing to give Vimal support. Another panel member from Leicester Property Services has helped with finding him premises, and is still supporting him by helping to find bigger premises. This aspect of finding temporary teams to support entrepreneurs is a fundamental component of the BizFizz approach – let the enterpreneurs focus on those aspects of the business they enjoy, and help them develop networks of support to complement their skills.

Vimal's company Sweet Earth is now providing a comprehensive selection of products suitable for all ages, including babies. It sources its produce from local farmers and also imports a large variety of fruits, vegetables and other pre-packed products from organic fair trade sources abroad, most of them not available in the UK. They also deliver boxes of organic food to people's door and are now challenging local schools and hospitals to buy local and organic as well. In short, Sweet Earth is a success.

Vimal is successful partly because of his imagination, hard work and attention to detail. But he is also successful because of *who* he knows and the critical broad networks of support and advice that he has accessed – and now builds for himself. "We are as much friends as suppliers," he says about his customers. "It is really good when you are a small business or a small farmer to work with people you can trust."

Those initial networks are so important for new entrepreneurs, and this chapter is about how BizFizz tries to forge them.

One of the most important elements of a local BizFizz operation is a panel of 20 to 30 people that acts as a network for new entrepreneurs, helping them unblock problems and providing key information and contacts. This is definitely not a management committee, but an advice and networking group. It consists of well-connected and experienced people from the community and the wider area who can make a practical contribution.

Each panel member introduces the coaches to their personal networks, thus helping them to widen their contact with potential entrepreneurs, and to gain an overview of skills and resources that are available locally. The panel includes local people with different backgrounds: community leaders and activists, head teachers, faith group leaders, councillors, local entrepreneurs and business people from the wider area; people with expertise in key areas such as IT, marketing, book-keeping, premises, bankers and other finance providers; people from regulatory authorities such as planning, environmental health and the Inland Revenue.

What brings them together is a mutual passion for the area where they live and work. The ability to unleash local expertise and resources is the main difference between BizFizz and other business support. That is why panel members are asked to contribute not only in their professional role, but using all their personal experience and knowledge. For example, local panels are very helpful with finding premises, identifying waste materials that can be used by other businesses, and linking entrepreneurs with common interests.

There are networks beyond the local panel as well, and not just those known to the panel members. To make a local BizFizz project work requires a local partner organisation which can promote the project, and act as a manager and employer of the coach. In all the BizFizz projects, a small number of local organisations and individuals have got together to form local management groups. These are not like big regeneration partnerships or voluntary sector management committees, but a small group which provides a link between the project and the community, giving guidance and support to the coach and the national BizFizz team on local issues. By dealing with the management of the project. It frees the local panel to concentrate on practical help to entrepreneurs.

That gives panel meetings a fascinating flavour. In my areas, Belgrave Heartlands and Latimer, we hold the panel meetings from 11 am to 1 pm, because this is the most suitable time for most of the members. Venues are offered by panel members at no cost, and they usually also supply tea, coffee, water and biscuits. Over the years, I have gotten to know the panel members really well. They could potentially earn a great deal per hour, but they have chosen to give us two hours a month, and they are enormously creative and focused on the nitty-gritty detail of solutions.

We usually wait five minutes to make sure no-one misses the first question from a client – and the best way we find is to formulate the advice they need as a specific question that the panel can get their teeth into. We start with the first client's question, which I present to the panel myself. This one is about local promotion: "When you get the free newspaper delivered, do you look at the fliers within? If not, why not? What would encourage you to give them your attention?"

This is the question that really helped the client focus on the choice of paper for delivering fliers. We also found out during discussion that a successful competitor used the same method.

It is time for the second question. This client is passionate about electronic music: he has varied experience of the industry and has produced more than 500 tracks. He believes that groups that are producing electronic music, whether they are young or old, often need support for the production process. So the question is: how can he access enough of these groups to be able to create a viable social enterprise?

The client told the panel that he had enrolled on a short media course – originally suggested by one of the panel members – which helped him make new contacts in the industry, but he had also decided that setting up a social enterprise might not be what he really wanted to do. I later got in touch with a member of their wider network who works for the Arts Council, and who advised him to spend some time checking the record producers by reading record labels of similar types of music and then sending samples of his work to them.

After the second question, we have a quick recap of client activities from the previous month's meeting. I want to make sure they know that their advice has been valuable, to let them know which of their ideas the client actually carried out and what had happened as a result. If there is a new member on the panel, we usually do brief introductions at this time, too. Then on to the next questions.

The third client will be offering organisations IT support and bespoke IT systems. His question is about marketing strategies: "How would you as business people react to letters, phone calls or emails as the best way to approach you?" He also asks:

- What information do you want to see?

- What kind of business press do you read?

- Do you have an IT support team? Or do you outsource?

- Would you spend time answering a questionnaire?

As a result of the advice he gets, the client later altered his marketing strategy. The panel came up with some excellent ideas and, even more importantly, this information was useful to several clients later on.

Lunch has usually arrived by now and, if we are celebrating the success of a new start-up, we have a toast to that business at this stage. I always use small businesses to supply the food for lunch – and from BizFizz clients if I can – as we can showcase their foods as well as their fliers and contact details. Panel members are able to network and add further information to the panel questions of the day as they chat over lunch. We finish promptly at 1 pm. The informal network has grown a little more, and more connections have been made.

Unlike some of the local BizFizz projects, our local panel is largely made up of people from outside Belgrave. But they all know the Belgrave area, and some of them are from agencies that are able to refer local clients to me. I also believe that having outside contacts has reinforced my neutrality in what can be a divided environment.

In practice, it has been very difficult to get people from within the local community involved. There is a great deal of local competitiveness here and a belief you have to make it by yourself, and certainly never go asking others for help, except from those close to you. There was an initial reluctance to get involved by some of the locals. I approached local businesspeople, but often their response was: "Your clients need to make the same mistakes we did." For those who did want to get involved, lack of time was an issue. "We all know how this works, Natalia," said one individual. "You scratch my back; I'll scratch yours."

I had to tell them: "Actually, I don't scratch backs!"

So the embattled sense of the local business community and the expectations of back-scratching both conspired to mean we had to reach further away to create the supportive networks we needed. But that had benefits, too. One of the benefits of being connected to broader networks is that it gave us a more balanced and more rooted approach. But there was another benefit, too. Some of my clients have aspirations for their business that are much wider. They often want a market beyond Belgrave and see our network as a way of giving them access and advice from this wider world.

The panel, and the networks it connects to, may not be the critical determinant of success for my clients. They probably would have achieved the same without their help, but it would certainly have taken them longer. The network helps to speed things up. It links people to contacts that might be relevant to each business and it brings the whole process forward.

The network has also helped me in my work as a BizFizz coach. With their support, I need not feel so alone in supporting my clients. I have the panel and wider network, and I also have the national BizFizz team The people that I have asked to be on my network are also incredibly approachable. I can ask them questions at the oddest times of the day or night, most often by email with the occasional phone call.

When I tell my clients that I have this network behind me, they can see BizFizz is more than just one person working on their behalf. Some of them now ask if their questions can be presented to the panel, rather than waiting for me to suggest it. And if the panel might not have the answers, there is a wider group behind them that I can dip into if necessary.

I have people in my network that I don't necessarily invite onto the panel. This is for a variety of reasons, often because they cannot commit to the required time or just don't fit easily into the dynamics of the meetings. I contact them immediately if I need something and it is extraordinary how it works. My clients think my phone is an oracle: I have all these contacts in it. I call people when I'm with them and they can see how quickly people respond.

Apart from simple advice, the panel members have helped clients in very practical ways, too. They have produced client branding at a special rate, and given extra time so that they really understood the clients' needs and concerns. They have found business premises and gone along with the client's to see them to make sure the client's particular requirements could be met. They have provided information on insurance policies and given quotations – but also explained that clients were likely to find more economical options with other companies. They have helped sort out problems with benefits and given legal advice to help prevent one client from being deported. They have arranged for a client to visit a school to test out their meditation book for children.

They have also given advice on taxation – and offered the names of smaller and cheaper accountants. They have commissioned work, displayed business cards and brochures, and even distributed flyers in their building. That is valuable support, but it is their friendly advice – their commitment to the project and to the efforts of the people who live locally – that is absolutely invaluable.

We began with a panel of four. By the time we met for the second time, it had grown to eight members and now I get between fourteen and sixteen every meeting. Within that number, there is a regular core, joined by different people every month. They offer to host it and provide us with hot drinks.

I would like to get clients onto the panel, but I am struggling. They tend to be too busy, or sometimes too nervous. They agree and then have to pull out because of work commitments. Also I suspect that, for some, it can be hard to see panel members who have helped them as their peers. They are, of course, and I also believe it is enormously important that their own experience gets fed back to the next entrepreneurs starting up. I hope this will begin to happen increasingly after the initial BizFizz project is over, because mutual support is vital to the genuine regeneration of this area.

And when they do, and the network continues after the end of the project – and after I have gone – I do have some advice for them, and for anyone else who wants to start a panel along these lines. There are a few guidelines that apply to BizFizz local panels, just as they apply to their equivalent anywhere else, and they include the following:

Be creative rather than judgemental.

I held a panel induction at the beginning. One person turned up late. He had missed the question at the beginning, but kept interrupting and not allowing anyone else to speak. In practice, he was failing to focus either on the client or on any potential solution, and I found it very difficult to get other people back into the discussion.

After that, I decided I needed to take more care about who I invited to be on the panel. I make sure I meet each new potential panel member. I do a small induction to make sure they understand what is expected of them and something about the BizFizz ethos. I show them the BizFizz presentation on my laptop. I explain the purpose of the meetings and I look for sincerity and an understanding of the BizFizz values. I also get a feel for what they can offer.

I usually find that the people I select for the panel have been involved in business in some way. I never say 'no' to anyone, but I select people either to be on the panel or act as part of my wider network. Sometimes people are just not able to commit to two hours a month. But I try to make everyone feel important, because I know – at some stage – they could be very valuable to one of my clients.

Co-operate with anyone.

I have had a great deal of support from agencies that do not appear to feel threatened by BizFizz. They include Community Action Network (CAN), Skills for Enterprise (formerly the Centre for Enterprise), BIG Bus Initiative Guidance and LACBA (Leicester African Caribbean Business Association) and Helping Hands. There are those who are not usually able to offer the same kind of support as we can, like Revenue and Customs, Job Centre Plus and Leicester Property Services. The CIRT (Creative Industries) team for the cultural quarter also offers information on events to support design, art and media-type businesses. Other agencies are happy to recommend, but very rarely meet clients who do not meet their criteria.

There are some other organisations that, in practice, are not very forth-coming in directing and referring clients. They are also rather posses-sive of the clients they have, so you have to be a little wary. But taken together, the broader the network – and the wider the variety of people and organisations involved – the more supportive it can be.

The key is to realise that there are shared goals: the regeneration of the local economy and opportunities for local inhabitants. People have to take a leap of imagination sometimes to realise that if entrepreneurs succeed, everyone benefits, but once they understand that, they help where they can.

Make it fun.
Our panel members say they enjoy the meetings. They say we have created a comfortable, even a humorous atmosphere. I believe that is true and, if so, it has certainly encouraged creativity. But the bottom line is that it is good fun. One panel member said: "Give me the next three dates in advance, Natalia; I don't want to miss one of them."

They all take pleasure from knowing they have helped someone. I deliberately start the meeting by getting straight into the first two questions, but then I always make sure I recap on how businesses are doing after their advice. They prefer general conversation rather than working just between individuals: they like to build on each other's ideas and they are also good at giving each other a turn to speak.

But then I think they learn something, too. I have had panel members who have been so inspired by my clients that they have decided to start businesses themselves. Two have even become clients.

Be positively naïve.
The most important lesson I have learned – and this may be the most important lesson to learn from networking – is that I definitely don't have all the answers. That means I have to create a positive atmos-phere at the panel meetings, to encourage people to contribute if they possibly can. I might add things to the list if I think the panel members missed something, but I never say 'we've already thought of that'. On the other hand, if we had thought of it before and tried it unsuccessful-ly, then I ask for additional information and extra opinions.

Even so, the panel come up with ideas that I would never have thought of. They think laterally in a way I never could. Sometimes the ideas can seem outrageous, but then we look at it again and think: maybe they are right.

At the beginning I was very anxious, particularly at the panel induction, but once I had become used to the meetings, I felt more relaxed. I think that was because I enjoyed the people so much. In fact, it didn't feel like work at all. I was having a brilliant time. As I identified how the panel best liked to work together, I became more of a facilitator. I always give sincere feedback. I allow time for them to develop their ideas. They stay focused on solutions, and if they start to analyse the business, I remind them gently that this is not what we are all here for. They get very limited client information – only what they need to answer the questions.

These four guidelines for running panels may not cover everything, but if you stick to them, the chances are that they will produce something creative and enjoyable.

My work with BizFizz is coming to an end and I am looking at how the networks can continue and build on the work we have done. I would like to broaden the work to involve other agencies in Leicester, like Skills for Enterprise (S4E), the Federation of Small Businesses and others. The aim is to set up a programme of networking meetings that BizFizz clients, as well as those of CAN and S4E, will be able to attend. This will provide them with an opportunity to meet other agencies and like-minded individuals. But the best outcome would be if the clients were to form a new network of people to bounce ideas off, and have new contacts to interact with.

There are opportunities for networking for local business already. In the Belgrave area, there is an entrepreneurs' network called ESP, or Entrepreneurs Striving in Partnership. For a subsidised annual fee of £100, it offers a monthly dinner at different venues with speakers, which is a brilliant opportunity for its members. But most of my clients have no access to transport, even if they could afford the fee, so the different venues could be problematic. The real problem is that few of them feel they are 'proper' businesses yet and do not usually feel this kind of event is for them.

So some kind of networking legacy is important, to continue support for entrepreneurs and to help incubate new clients, so that they can start slowly with the support they need to succeed. What we need is a facilitator willing to co-ordinate meetings, and to make sure the questions will be focused on solutions. We also need a budget to finance this co-ordinator or event manager.

There are other resources around, lying unused, if we can find ways of bringing them back into use. There is no shortage of suitable buildings being neglected which have character and would encourage visitors, and would be perfect as business incubation units. What we need – and not just in my neighbourhood – is people in towns and cities with open minds who can see the potential of local people, local networks and unused buildings, and with enough imagination to bring those together, preferably with a budget and some staffing.

The point is that in Belgrave, and indeed the city of Leicester, there are enormous resources to be tapped. There is imagination and know-how among the people who live there. There is their combined spending power and the unused buildings lying empty in public ownership. There is also the powerful resources of support and advice once some of those people get together.

The potential of networks to make things possible has become one of the most important lessons for me from the whole BizFizz experience. In the remaining time I have running this project, I am concentrating on networking events. I am running as many of them as I can so that clients have other like-minded people to listen to them, advise them and support them – and build for themselves a supportive network.

Businesses can be very insular. Some businesses, especially in the areas where I work, can get by just by continuing to supply the same customers and have little ambition to do anything else. That is fine and it works for some businesses. There are also many other small businesses that want to be more adventurous, are interested to see what is going on outside their immediate circle, and would really value more networking. Even so, they may not be good at introducing themselves to other people. They are probably uncomfortable about actually asking for help or advice. For them, networks of support – which allow them to do these things relatively painlessly, and in such a way that they can learn a great deal – are absolutely invaluable.

It is hardly surprising that small business networking clubs are experiencing a massive explosion all over the country. They are deliberately not industry specific. They range from the informal to the high-class – like the famous First Tuesday events that powered the dot.com revolution – and they work because they are face-to-face, human and potentially supportive. We have been pioneering a way of doing that to encourage new entrepreneurs, and have discovered from experience that it works.

Interlude: BizFizz client, Thetford

"I see a small place. I don't want something big. A small place is enough. In Portugal I worked six years at that. Then I came here and I saw an opportunity, and I knew the job.

I knew what I wanted and since I found Ali (the BizFizz coach), she gave me more confidence in what I was doing. Now I want to set up a café Portuguese patisseries. Ali knew what I wanted and tried to help me in every way I can see. If it wasn't for BizFizz or Ali, I would never come like I am now here.

Alone, I tried to ask for some money from the banks to start up and I tried to find some partners, but I couldn't get through. Sometimes I just let go. When someone says no to you, you don't want to carry on.

So I quit, until I found Ali, and I don't want to quit now because I have her support now and the BizFizz support. I want to open a patisserie with BizFizz help, and everything goes fine except for these premises, but – like Ali says – you just have to keep looking. So that's what I am doing.

We are immigrants, so most people don't want to help us. It's special when you find someone who cares about the work; who actually really, really wants to help."

Fatima Largo Ribeiro

Chapter 6
From within

Mark Shipperlee

'While we humans observe and count separate selves, and pay
a great deal of attention to the differences that seem to divide
us, in fact we survive only as we learn how to participate in a
web of relationships.'
Margaret Wheatley, Leadership & the New Science

'You can't argue with something that works.'
**David Eccles,
Head of Regeneration, Bolsover District Council
and member of Clowne local management group**

There is an abandoned hotel owned by a large estates company outside Alnwick, where I have been working as a BizFizz coach. It is on
the very edge of the national park and looking across the Cheviot
Hills. It is also near a small village, and has been renovated some
years ago, but was never actually re-opened, either as a hotel or as
anything else. I never quite understood why not. It is built with sand-
stone and it stands an impressive three storeys high, in a beautiful
spot with the hills in the distance. In a region like ours, recovering from
the closure of the pits and trying to attract tourists, it really should not
still be going to waste.

One of my clients has been a former deputy headteacher with plans
for a new language school, teaching students who are on their way to
university in the UK to become doctors or lawyers or take other professional courses. It is an ambitious and professional plan and it means
ten new jobs, five of them locals and five more attracting in outsiders
to the area. But we have found it difficult to persuade the estate that
owned the building to end its long vacancy, and help play a useful
role in the local economy again. After a long silence, I wrote to the
property owners myself, but no matter what I said, they simply would
not discuss the lease. As a result, the building has sat empty for
another year. Those ten jobs are also badly needed in Alnwick.

That is symptomatic of one of the peculiarities and paradoxes of the area I've been working in. It is supposed to provide the best quality of life in the UK, according to GMTV and *Country Living* magazine and the house prices are soaring, yet it is also impoverished, rather isolated and near a number of former coalfields. It has resources in the form of empty buildings, and considerable regeneration funds pouring into the region nearby, yet it suffers from distant regeneration bureaucracies and old-fashioned landlords – like the hotel owners – who seem semi-detached and rather sluggish.

The truth is that rural regeneration is not very visible in the north of Northumberland. Further down the coast, money has been poured into the areas that were affected when the collieries closed. We did get one big injection of money after foot and mouth blitzed the communities, which was intended to help farmers to diversify. The psychological effect from huge loss of livestock and bonfires of carcases has been quite profound here. But, although we get little of their money, we do get six layers of government structures that cover the region. There is central government, the regional development agency, sub-regional partnerships, the county council, district council and town council. With all this support you would think that change would happen quickly. The reality is that the effect of all this top-down interventions, delivered by distant agencies, makes people feel impotent and bewildered. They have little idea what is going on. Most people just accept the status quo of 'being done to'. They have little sense sometimes that there are any channels in existence whereby they can change things themselves.

Part of the problem is that there are undoubtedly hidden structures in the area that maintain the status quo in all kinds of ways. There are peculiar 'old boys networks'. Many decisions happen away from the public table and behind closed doors. North Northumberland is in many ways still a feudal society. A few families own vast tracts of land and a handful of individuals appear to own most of the property in Alnwick town. I have come to realise that the reason why there are many underused shops in the area is that the people who own them simply don't need the rent money. There is a café by the sea that has stayed empty for well over a year. It is a golden opportunity for a new business, but potential entrepreneurs feel exhausted at the thought – not of running a successful business – but the hurdles they would need to leap through just to get a decision made about leasing the property.

There are certainly obstacles to regeneration in Alnwick, and – after networking hard there for the past two years – there is still a great deal of this puzzle we have yet to understand. What we have understood is that, whatever the obstacles, there is a wealth of imaginative spirit and entrepreneurial people here – as there is everywhere – and they have begun to reinvigorate the town and its surroundings. And, in doing so, they have begun to challenge the top-down model of regeneration which assumes that it is something done by outsiders. Real development, as we know, happens from within.

So it is worth taking a second look at Alnwick, one that goes below the surface of these institutional structures into the heart of the community, where there are people who want things to happen, and have ideas and imagination. Many of them are incomers to the area, though many of them are not. Those newcomers include people who have come up to north Northumberland because it is a beautiful part of the country and they want to set up a new life. Unlike some rural areas, there is no suspicion of incomers here. People are happy to let them get on and do whatever they want. Many of them have become BizFizz clients and seem to be bringing new energy to the place.

BizFizz has also added an important new ingredient. It gives people an opportunity to come and talk about an idea without being judged. It provides local networking opportunities with other entrepreneurs and a great deal of inter-trading takes place. This is particularly important in an area which is geographically isolated, where starting-up or running a small business can feel like a very solitary option. But it provides a wide-ranging agenda to link people up across a breadth of disciplines and sectors, which large agencies are often constrained from doing.

As the BizFizz coach, I had a free agenda to meet people, to go and see the pub owner, solicitor, accountant, surveyor, postmaster and many others who might be able to help remove barriers facing my clients. So I have done a lot of linking people together, which is so vital in dispersed rural communities where people can feel personally isolated, and there is now a collection of people here who are bumping into each other, all interested in getting things done.

One major innovation which is changing the local economy is the opening of Alnwick Gardens. At the height of last year's season, a quarter of the people who visited left the gardens through the exit that led to Alnwick town. The Gardens have been a great success and there are many opportunities for businesses in the vicinity: hotels, bike hire shops, tea rooms and other attractions that could bring income into the local economy, and feed back in visitor numbers. The gardens are not big enough to hold the attention of visitors for a complete day, and most people who come from outside the area to visit the gardens will come for the weekend. So Alnwick's challenge is how to make the most of this opportunity and increase how much visitors spend in the town during their stay.

Alnwick Gardens is a home-grown initiative. But regeneration from within the community makes the role of the BizFizz coach different from the equivalent in a government agency. We have to listen and collect people and talk: that's what being a catalyst is all about. But it is sometimes a difficult concept for traditional agencies to understand. We never go out with a good idea and persuade people to carry it out, though sometimes we have to help adjusting someone else's idea to a more realistic level. Someone came to us who wanted to start an eco-community, and after working with them for some time, they have now launched a mushroom farming business. We had to learn a great deal about mushrooms, and the first crop is due any time now. The eco-community might happen, too, but we had to help identify the best place to begin.

Nor do we even go out to identify likely entrepreneurial individuals. They have to find us. Apart from a network of contacts in the community, we don't even have a sign outside the BizFizz office in Alnwick, which is on the first floor of a rural surveyor's office. There are added challenges for this kind of development from within when you are in a rural area. People are more isolated. Childcare is that much more difficult. If you have one car and your partner needs it for work, then you will probably need another car – you certainly can't rely on public transport. The nearest photocopier might be fifteen miles away, and within the same radius as someone living in a city, there is a very much smaller potential market.

We tackled a small part of this problem by buying an A3 printer, laminator and comb-binder. We encourage people to use the internet more, both for buying and selling, to get a wider market. It means we have to travel more ourselves, meeting in people's homes or in pubs, or meeting up for breakfast or very late at night.

But the proof of development from within lies in the fact that, despite all these difficulties, people with passion and ideas track us down. They range from the man who started selling computers on eBay as a business to the nurse with depression who wanted to start a wedding dress business. The first man is now very successful, the second opened a wedding dress shop in November 2004 and has now bought another wedding business in a nearby seaside town.

Alnwick Gardens have been very supportive towards BizFizz and several BizFizz clients have included the Gardens when they planned their product placement. The opportunity to focus attention on this growing number of visitors has created a buzz amongst local entrepreneurs. We also have other wonderful tourist attractions, such as the Farne Islands, the coastline and a national park. But top-down thinking does not necessarily help the emerging enterprises in Alnwick to capitalise on this.

One North East, the local regional development agency, has had the remit for tourism for a year and a bit. So far, they have run an £15-million branding campaign and are now starting to create four area tourism partnerships which will cover Northumberland, County Durham, Teesside and Tyne and Wear. These new partnerships can often mean more institutionalised structures, hidebound by targets, procedures and meetings, unaware of what is needed on the ground. In practice, I have found that this top-down approach means little or nothing to the local guesthouse owners. They are more concerned with the practical side of making sure there is a good bus and train service for their customers. There are local associations of B&B owners, but they tend to be bewildered. They have little idea about the plans of One North East for tourism and no idea how they can feed into them.

This top-down approach does little to support local entrepreneurs in the tourism industry to spot gaps in the market or provide for locally specific needs. This requires support and decision-making to be actually within a community, not inflicted on it from on high. Yet there are dynamic individuals out there, even in the public sector. Some of them, in particular, are working in the county council to find ways of increasing the way local money flows around the local economy.

Conventional thinking in regeneration, which is inevitably top-down, imagines that somehow their only task is to bring investment into an area, forgetting that – if there is not a strong local base of businesses and suppliers – that money will simply flow away again to other areas. But there are things that the public sector can do about this. They have enormous purchasing powers, and there should be ways that they can open up the opportunities for local business to tender for these contracts, by making the process more accessible and reducing the size of the contract so a small firm can deliver it – for food in schools or hospitals, for example.

For one thing, this will reduce the amount of energy used and pollution produced trucking goods in from outside the region. For another, it means that these resources can be used to develop the neglected areas nearer home, and the money can circulate around the local economy, allowing local entrepreneurs to develop sustainable local businesses.

One of those working on this issue is Adam Wilkinson formally from Northumberland County Council, one of the original members of the BizFizz local management group. He worked in partnership with **nef** to apply a measurement tool called LM3, to see the impact Northumberland County Council procurement decisions have on the local economy by tracking where their money is spent and re-spent from procurement contracts.

The project was a great success and this approach has now been adopted by the North East Centre for Excellence, which is working with all 25 local authorities in the north east to challenge how they procure their goods and services, and drawing out the regeneration impact of their procurement decisions. Northumberland found that measuring money flows led to greater efficiency in the public sector, whilst becoming a major component of how change happens by benefiting the broader local economy and the businesses operating there. Northumberland itself is now aiming to spend ten per cent more of their procurement budget locally, in the belief that this extra ten per cent will mean an extra £35 million invested in the local economy.

Northumberland put out one tender recently for grass-cutting and maintenance. But, instead of tendering in one giant block – which only a few companies could fulfil – they broke it down into small blocks so that businesses could tender for smaller geographical areas. The tendering process turned out to be still quite daunting when you approached it for the first time, but the county council offered useful one-to-one advice sessions. We worked with one BizFizz client and we put together a really good tender document, making sure the client had all the correct safety and environmental policies in place. As a result, they won one of the local grass-cutting contracts.

There is a great deal more that can be done along these lines to get the life back into the local economies. Development from within is a challenging business. It means that local people have be proactive to demand change and take action to make that change. That can be frightening – for all those involved – but it is also potentially transformative. Yet bottom-up regeneration is attracting increased interest because it actually works. It shifts attitudes and it is close enough to the people with the imagination and passion to create real change.

Development of any BizFizz project comes from residents who want to do something. But that does not mean that we simply have to sit back and wait for something to happen. In previous programmes, we often had initial conversations with two or three people who – for whatever reason – had a passion for enterprise and for local entrepreneurial success. These people then spread the word, find support from business and local activists, recruit some panel members and then raise funds to pay for a coach and join together to form the local management group.

This group provides a number of functions in the project. We ask that the coach be free to operate 100 per cent with clients, not to join committees or partnerships or write funding bids or strategies. The group then provides the strategic link in the project: it looks at strategic barriers affecting the clients – if there is no business space, or lack of financial support available to an area, for example. Its role is about removing barriers to people who care enough to pursue a solution. And, in the end, this passion can only be evoked from within a community.

The four very entrepreneurial people who came together to set up the BizFizz local management group had never worked together before. There was Adam Wilkinson, who was then head of social enterprise at Northumberland County Council. There was Kate Potts, a business consultant with a special interest in food and marketing. Also Mikyla Robinson, one of the initiators of BizFizz, then working for the

Community Council Northumberland, and Ian Brown, a farmer who has diversified into other businesses.

They really seemed to spark off each other, and very quickly began to realise the barriers to development from within that they were up against. Ian Brown showed us a map of the Northumberland 'agency landscape' which showed how about 55 different agencies – the equivalent of middlemen – soaked up so much of the funding that is supposed to help develop the region before it got near the residents of the area. We realised very quickly that it is so complicated and confusing to navigate this map that most people give up.

As a result of working together on BizFizz, three of the local management group – plus me – have set up a not-for-profit company called Local Living. You might ask, given the existing 55 agencies, whether Northumberland needs another, but development from within requires a voice, and our challenge is to remain true to those values. Our mission statement is: to benefit the residents of north Northumberland by facilitating local money flows and catalysing the development of profitable social and private enterprises.

We want to try and get the idea of buying local more widespread and, to support this, we bid for and won the market licence in Alnwick, to reinvigorate the market in this tradition market town – offering the opportunity to BizFizz and other entrepreneurs to set up regular stalls. So when visitors leave Alnwick Gardens, they can come and experience all this local food and produce from the surrounding area. We also want to take over a building in the town and convert it into workspace for small businesses, possibly with an art café and exhibition space, and there is nowhere obvious for this to be yet. As a result, we are having to challenge the local status quo. But the idea is to be a catalyst: it is development from within that works and it has a kind of energy of its own.

We have networked hard with BizFizz over the last two years and got to know a lot of people. We have met and talked to property owners, lawyers, development trust directors and board members. We have come to know people from the local authority and trustees of voluntary organisations. We have sought out those who see the value of BizFizz connections. And because we are on the spot, we can talk to them in a way that the distant agencies are simply unable to do.

The editor of the local paper has agreed to publish a monthly article about BizFizz clients. One of the leading lawyers in the town agreed to give a half-hour free advice session to a BizFizz client, and afterwards indicated a willingness to do it again. Local accountants will look over cash flows and pass back advice for clients. Estate agents watch out for property for us. All this support has proved absolutely invaluable. People are starting to say the magic words: "If I can be of help, please get in touch." We have watched a bank manager change a client's credit score so that they can get the short-term loan they needed, because through our supportive network they can trust all those involved. In short, there is a growing positive attitude towards local entrepreneurs in the community – and doors are starting to open.

Interlude – How to create an excellent local management group

BizFizz local management groups are the groups of people who have accepted local responsibility for the management and strategic direction of each project – and I've seen a number of them in operation. Each project begins at the same point – understanding, endorsing and committing to work with the values and working model that is BizFizz. But after that, I've noticed that there are common factors that seem to underlie their success.

The mix: The group will include the person who started the project whether they are local entrepreneurs, from local authorities, development trusts, or anywhere else. But the group also needs to include people living and working in the area. They ground the project and act as a barometer of change. Often it will include people who have never met before, and the effective group will have to think strategically and act practically – so it helps to include creative 'big thinkers' and pragmatic 'completer finishers'.

The values: To be truly effective, the local management group must reflect the values of BizFizz in the way it operates. Members need to allow the project to gather its own pace, supporting the coach during the first few months, referring clients and opening up their own networks to them. They also need to understand the role of coach and the need for freedom and flexibility – the only question they really need to ask is: how does this benefit the clients? They also need to be attracted by a common desire to effect change and believe that this is the way to do so – not because they have been sent, or because they want to keep an eye on the competition.

Each local management group is asked to put together a list of local success criteria. This enables the group to go beyond using statistics as a measure, and to articulate other measures that will be important for them. The chair and instigator of the Winsford local management group, Gary Cliffe, said that he would like to hear one person say: "BizFizz changed my life".

Some months later he called in a local tradesman to do some work at his home. Neither knew the other was involved in BizFizz. Asking how the business was going, Gary was told that it had been having serious difficulties because of seasonal fluctuations in demand. But having been referred to the BizFizz coach by the Citizen's Advice Bureau, things had really turned around. "Meeting with Vicki saved my business," he said – so Gary got his wish.

The host: Each project has a host organisation that agrees to take on responsibility for 'pay and rations'. Their representative sits on the local management group, but has an equal voice and accepts that overall management of the coach and the project lies with the collective local management group. This works best when these organisations are able to accept this 'cuckoo in the nest' arrangement, not having the need to place any organisational demands on the coach.

The actions: A great local management group can really add value to the project. Adopting an entrepreneurial attitude, they become champions and their actions can change local policy and practice.

Client feedback in Clowne showed a lack of business start-up space. Top-down solutions of creating business parks and incubator space in the cities had not really worked for local residents, who did not want to take on this amount of travel. Rather than accept that the strategy was not working, the assumption was made that there weren't many entrepreneurs in the town. The Clowne local management group, with support from the panel, have gone on to form a social enterprise to take on the renovation and management of a derelict building to meet this newly realised local demand.

The synergy: With the energy of a great local management group, BizFizz becomes the catalyst for local change. In Winsford, the success of the project has led to one of the group, David Horstead, making it part of the Warrington and Cheshire's future economic strategy. "In these 'enterprise cold spots' we find enormous barriers to turning dreams into reality," it says. "Many residents have no experience of trade and commerce, no obvious access to funding – and above all a lack of confidence about taking the plunge. Our existing support agencies are very good, but often we find that people in these 'cold spots' are too nervous to approach business advisors."

The BizFizz local management groups play a pivotal part in changing the collective consciousness of an area and making the shift towards a thriving and enterprising community.

Lynne Jones
National Co-ordinator, BizFizz

Chapter 7
The challenge

Elizabeth Cox

"If we talk of promoting development, what have we in mind – goods or people?"

E.F. Schumacher

"You see things, and you say, 'Why?' But I dream things that never were, and I say, "Why not?"

George Bernard Shaw

"We can do no great things; only small things with great love."

Mother Teresa

An over emphasis on inward investment, and a belief that you can build your way out of deprivation, with little or no thought for how this investment links in with local firms and local people's aspirations, has meant that regeneration over the last 20 years has failed to deliver the sought for change in communities experiencing economic disadvantage. BizFizz points a way to a new kind of regeneration – and for me its lessons pose some fundamental questions for the starting points, and focus of development initiatives, questions which we are now beginning to explore in some of our other work.

- What would the world look like if people were permitted to follow their dreams?

- What would the support system look like if it was 100% client-focused, and supported people to remove barriers that stood in the way of their success?

- If targets were replaced by values as drivers for initiatives – what would values-based regeneration look and feel like?

- If central government, regional development agencies, local authorities and other support agencies became learning organisations, involving their clients as equal partners in that reflective practice – how would this impact on power relations and well-being across society?

At some point in regeneration thinking people became the problem rather than being seen as a resource; they were described only in terms of statistics of deprivation. The physical community became the focus of the intervention to improve the economy, as opposed to the human community in the area. The thinking behind this appears to be that if the physical infrastructure is provided, everything else would follow with community development there to deal with social problems. I am indebted to Edgar Cahn and his influential work on Timebanks for his insight into how this impacts on people's behaviour – people know how to grow their assets and if the only way that you are recognised is by your problems then this becomes how you refer to yourself if there is no motivation to talk about the positive contributions that you bring. This eventually erodes self-belief, leading to a downward cycle of dis-empowerment.

Regeneration has spawned a veritable industry of professional problem finders – 'the experts' who know what is best. In this world, participation is reduced to consultation – you can choose what you would like as long as it is from our pre-selected list of options. Somewhere in the avalanche of agencies with a professional interest in the problems of deprivation the human element is overlooked – resourceful, creative people who do not benefit from being defined by the negatives ascribed to the place where they live.

Institutionalising regeneration also brings with it institutional patterns of behaviour – solutions must be replicable across communities, approaches must be administratively efficient to deliver. Issues become projectised and mechanistic in their approach, and priority is given to those issues that can be packaged in this way. There is assumed to be a straight-line causal relationship between problem and solution – the professionals identify the problem, opt for a solution, break this into activities, box it into a time line, calculate needed resources to deliver activities. The world becomes a simplified logical framework of analysis – the task of supporting change is reduced to one of delivering the project, implying that change can be ordered and delivered like fast-food. This planned approach is based upon the premise that social change can be engineered and directed – produced at will.[2] The human element – the possibility of the unusual,

creativity, innovation, dreams, aspirations, drivers, personal choice –
has no place in this construct.

The end result of this is the profesionalisation[3] of regeneration and
international development where people become objects – they are
beneficiaries – where statistics become the core descriptor of human
existence and define them as targets, or non-targets for support. If you
use the language of beneficiaries then you embed power relationships
in the project design - between the professionals and the subjects of
their profession. If you shape a persons experience as a subject – then
expect passivity to emerge. Yet it is this very passivity and apathy that
will continue to imprison communities in a downward cycle of *dis-
empowerment* – and so remain continual fodder for the professionals.

Couple this with the tendency of the experts within institutions, which
are at their heart risk averse, to become hidebound by rules and
requirements. Then I would argue that this is not the best starting
point to providing communities with support to become enterprising.

If there is to be sustainable change in communities experiencing economic disadvantage – then the regeneration sector has to find ways
to tap into the natural resourcefulness, skills and passions of the local
people. The key ingredient missing in regeneration initiatives to date is
to deliver support to communities as if people mattered – as opposed
to neat administrative constructs. For regeneration to rise to the challenge of supporting sustainable development requires a radical re-
thinking of core components of the present system.

Starting points – active choice
"Is there anyone out there who wants to do something"?

The opening question for a BizFizz project, and the one that sets the
tone of our approach – action from within the community, rather than
wish lists for change. Underlying this question is the power to decide
– it is an invitation to action. If regeneration and development initiatives are going to reverse the rising tide of apathy, disengagement
and dependency in communities experiencing economic disadvantage – then they need to have approaches which are actively sought
out by members of the community to be implemented in their area. A
prerequisite for this is that the initiatives must make practical sense,
and be relevant to the aspirations of that community.

Being invited into an area by members of the community gives enormous credibility to BizFizz locally. Many communities in the UK have been subjected to initiatives which have time and again been parachuted in by some faceless agency to mend their externally perceived deficits. Outreach and buy-in then become the two major hurdles these initiatives have to overcome – let alone being seen as relevant. From our BizFizz experience we have learnt that when a community actively chooses to have a project, is involved in the decision-making of recruiting key staff – in this case the BizFizz coach - and when the strategic management of the project is based in the community – these elements all serve to develop a sense of local ownership and responsibility for the project. This responsibility extends beyond the life of the initial project to developing the successor strategy, and continuing active engagement in challenging the economic status quo through action.

Placing enterprise at the heart of regeneration

BizFizz is a model focused on business support – however what we have observed over the past four years is that in addition to the sought for outcomes of additional business start-ups and jobs created, there is also an attitudinal shift in the communities that we have worked in. One that starts to see opportunities and solutions, is risk aware and prepared to take action – an attitude we would describe as enterprising. This is apparent not only in the passionate clients we have worked with, but also in our coaches, the local management group and the panel.

When we talk of enterprise being placed at the heart of regeneration, it is describing an attitude to life, as opposed to the somewhat narrow definition applied by government with respect to business. Through a focus on supporting entrepreneurs, bringing a group of people together to be solution focused to remove barriers faced by entrepreneurs from their local area, and celebrating the success of clients we are drawing upon enterprising behaviour to fuel a deeper and wider social change. A change that is driven from within a community, and one where the professionals involved only hold the client's agenda, as agreed by that client. The professional's role becomes supportive and practical – not seeking to create businesses or planning another's future.

Enterprise means people look at an empty building locally – one that might have become a symbol for the economic difficulties of the town – and see it instead as a resource. They might take a second look at their neighbours and see, not a rundown community in search of regeneration, but valuable skills, experience and assets.

Out of all the outcomes from our programme, I believe it is this attitudinal shift which is the vital component to sustainable change in communities facing economic disadvantage. Enterprise is the human dynamic that has been sadly ignored in regeneration practice. However, to support enterprise requires a complete re-thinking of project design and delivery. Instead of outputs required by the project, the structure of the project must be flexible to the outcomes desired by their clients. The complementary shift in thinking required from clients is that they have to be prepared to identify what they want to do, and be prepared to take action to achieve their stated goal.

Building networks of support

Should we interpret the message of BizFizz to be that business is good and the font of all regeneration? Enterprise and people pursuing their business dreams is part of a story of change. The role of local networks of support brings another important element to that story, one that we are only just beginning to understand.

A striking outcome from BizFizz has been the collaborative behaviour of entrepreneurs – not the ruthless competition model business is supposed to represent. In part we think this is a result of basing support within a community using a coaching approach. But in addition, it is a result of the feeling of support people gain from what may be strangers on the panel being prepared to support their success – and the boost in confidence and sense of being valued that this has brought the entrepreneurs.

In some cases this has led to clients joining the panel themselves to give something back, or being part of the troubleshooting wider network of support for the coach. What is important is that the motivation to be a part of the network comes from the client. Requiring clients to 'pay back' on the support they have received would undermine the drivers behind this very personal motivation – it would be somebody else's 'should' and unlikely to result in a long-term behaviour change. Drivers must come from within if a strong reciprocal relationship is to be maintained – a sense that these areas have become communities where *local* bonds people.

Finding passion

A prerequisite for the people we support in BizFizz is that they are passionate about their business idea. We do not give them an idea to be passionate about, nor do we provide a motivational service to maintain a sense of passion in the client. In addition, we ask the client to name that part of the business they are passionate about, and actively build networks of support – temporary teams – to deliver those other elements they are less passionate about. This being based on the understanding that it feels good to focus on what you enjoy, and if you enjoy it, you are more likely to succeed. It also builds awareness of all the elements of business, but does not require the entrepreneur to deliver them all alone.

Ultimately supporting someone's passion does mean that professionals have to give up their control role. They can no longer be the expert with attachment to outcomes. The outcomes become those of the client as they themselves assume responsibility for the change they have named as their goal. Projects would then have to be developed with structures that were flexible at the individual level at point of delivery. Structures that are capable of supporting the development of temporary teams where necessary. This requires a fundamental shift in approach, from focusing on what is not there and delivering a factory-training approach to supporting entrepreneurs, to focusing support on unleashing enterprise in its widest sense. Essentially regeneration would have to move from seeing people in need of repair, to delivering support on the entrepreneur's own terms.

This change would require institutions to develop internal structures that supported this flexibility – becoming outcome focused as opposed to target driven. Straight-line causality and simple approaches to project design would have to be replaced by dynamic systems approaches, unrestricted by artificial timelines.

Re-focusing on passion within communities, this essentially human and organic approach to change – one with an inbuilt driver – is the antidote to dependency. People can start to take control of their lives, and can do so by pursuing what they are passionate about.

Continuation vs catalyst

In BizFizz we have come to understand that we provide an opportunity to catalyse change – we are not the change, nor are we essential to continuing change after the initial project. BizFizz is 24 months of exploring a different approach with a community from which there will be a decision within a community as to what next. It may develop into something radically different, or continue using the approach – only the name is trademarked in the interests of maintaining consistency of what it stands for – and communities are encouraged to find a name for themselves to describe their approach. Again we believe that this reinforces a sense of ownership from within a community, and reflects our understanding about not developing dependent relationships – in this case between the local management group and BizFizz – and not assuming a position of power over a community.

We do, however, invite the communities to maintain a relationship with us at a policy level. That is, channelling information from the community to inform policy at the national level – this being the wider role of **nef** and the Civic Trust. We thus move from an implementation relationship to a policy influencing relationship with the local management group over time. We become part of their wider network of support, as they do ours – an equal relationship.

BizFizz places support at the heart of a community. It also opens up the opportunity for the future to be shaped as the community determines. Our interest is to continue to learn from each area. If regeneration initiatives are interested in understanding sustainable development, then their relationships with the communities need to evolve over time, rather than be severed because a project has finished. If organisations are to move on from the mechanistic world of performance monitoring and the power-laden judgement of success handed down by external consultants, to becoming learning organisations, then roles and timeframes in the learning process need to be radically re-assessed.

Breaking the language barrier

To support enterprise as a driver for change in a community requires fundamental changes not only in approaches, but also in the language of regeneration. We need to eradicate language which describes areas and communities by what they do not have. It is a short step, and one that is frequently taken by agencies, to move from describing the area in these terms, to describing the people from the area in the same way. It is a language which indicates there is something wrong with people; there is something missing; they need to be repaired, trained. This thinking then informs the types of initiatives that are developed and the manner in which they are applied.

This language is reinforced by targeted approaches which define 'eligibility' through disadvantage – encouraging the individual to adopt the labels of disadvantage to 'qualify' for support, and of course detailed monitoring systems which capture you in the statistical profile of needy or different. We also see language used which infers a passive role on individuals in communities involved in projects such as beneficiaries previously noted. Other than making a monumental assumption that the project delivers benefit to anyone, this language is symptomatic of the uneven power relationships within programmes between professionals and the targeted population.

The use of this language encourages a dependent response from the community. In fact, the more you can tell the agency how bad things are, the more you seem to be rewarded. This language reinforces perceptions and deepens misconceptions of the roots for sustainable change being in the hands of the professionals to deliver. Ultimately this language is counter-intuitive to the goal of many of these initiatives. Passivity, dependency, lack of vision and drive are the antithesis of enterprising. It is not without some consideration that we have opted for the term 'client' in BizFizz. The term 'client' for us implies an adult-to-adult relationship between the coach and the entrepreneur, one where the power relationship is even between the parties.

Empowerment is another of the words in regeneration that has done a lot to entrench the professionals' self-belief that they have the answers, that they improve the people they work with. Empowerment has been applied across a broad range of definitions, from giving political voice to what I believe is the most insidious use of the term in regeneration – that a project or person has the power, normally through training of some sort, to give power to another – the inference being that the person was in deficit prior to this. However, it also infers omnipotence on the part of the regeneration practitioner to give power – that must be some ego to live with.

BizFizz focuses on removing barriers that stand in the way of an entre-preneur's success. We believe people are whole and empowered. However, they face certain barriers which *dis*-empower them, and we have spent four years learning about their removal. This is a funda-mental difference in our starting points with the individuals we work with. We are not in the business of repairing people. Coaching starts from the position that people are creative, resourceful and whole – they are empowered. It is not the person that needs improving – but rather the system that introduces the *dis*- to empowerment. Taking the need-for-empowerment route focuses on perceived shortcomings of a person, whereas focusing on removing the *dis*- from empowerment challenges structures and systems of support.

At the outset of BizFizz we were faced with the observation that in communities facing economic disadvantage there was less visible evi-dence of entrepreneurial activity. So either there were less entrepre-neurs, or entrepreneurs were facing particular barriers in these areas which were system based. Opting for the latter premise, as explored in Chapter 1, we then set about developing an alternative system of sup-port based within the community. The success of BizFizz proves our hypothesis that rather than a people problem, it was the system of support that could not reach the entrepreneurs in these communities – both physically and due to the processes used. If we had believed that we had the power to empower others, then BizFizz as an approach would never have emerged.

Language is a signal. It can reinforce power relationships or liberate. An awareness of language should be a basic skill of any regeneration professional. Not, of course, to be confused with the cynical applica-tion of politically correct language which so haunts the political land-scape in the UK today – token gesture language which floats free of any beliefs or values.

Changing language is an easy but essential step towards positive change. However, this should be a reflection of values, which are then applied in practice, and with honesty.

From targets to values and learning organisations

Signing up to language is not enough; the challenge is to opera-tionalise these values.

Targets do not deliver change in communities; neither do they clarify the role of a regeneration professional. Targets are established for the benefit of the funder, not the client. A support agency then finds it has two clients in any initiative – the group receiving the support, and the funding agency. With a direct link to the financial survival of the agency, the funder's agenda takes precedent over that of the client. The pace of change required becomes that demanded by the funder.

BizFizz, first by default because we did not know at the outset what communities we would be working with which made the establishment of targets an absurdity, and then by design, when we saw the positive outcomes from having no targets to skew the coach–client relationship, operates with no targets. Instead, we focus on outcomes which incorporate local success criteria.

The argument for targets is that they provide a measure of performance and act as a motivator. If targets are removed, what then replaces them as the motivation to deliver? In BizFizz we have replaced targets with values. Key to any of the projects is the personal qualities of the coach. In coach recruitment what we are looking for in addition to experience of business and a broad range of business skills, is a good fit with the values of the BizFizz programme. Whilst skills can be honed with practice, values emerge from life experiences and beliefs. They are prime motivators and drivers for success, far more effective than any external target set by a funder.

The preceding chapters have highlighted our values: trust, being 100 per cent client-focused in our support, never motivating or initiating, respecting our clients as creative, resourceful and whole, and placing decision-making within the community. The coaches operate within this framework of values with maximum freedom. They also have no institutional façade to hide behind – they are placed within that community and develop a personal relationship to it and their clients.

What targets also give is a sense that outputs are predictable, so appearing to lessen risk and give a rationale for funding allocation. The world, however, is complex, and a simplification of reality does not make it reality. Adopting an action-learning approach to reflecting on the outcomes of practice is a key way for organisations to deal with the unpredictability of implementing flexible approaches to support. If agencies are to be successful in supporting regeneration, then thinking of the community as an adaptive and complex system[4] is the first step.

BizFizz's challenge is whether institutions can look within themselves and question what their systems are for, the ease of administration, or to support their clients. Our approach is not rocket science; it is simple – flexibly support people to do what they want to do, and draw on the resources close to them (in the community, in their own networks and a wider local network) to support them to do this. Simple, easily understandable, and adaptable to a community's individual development context. There are parallels to the outcomes of BizFizz in some of the emerging work on co-production in public services[5]: opportunities for personal growth, use of peer networks, leadership by people within the community. We look forward to seeing how the system will rise to the challenge, reinvent itself, become flexible and dynamic, to support the passion for change within communities.

---

2   See Escobar, A (1993) 'Planning' in W Sachs *The Development Dictionary – A Guide to Knowledge as Power.* Zed

3   Included in this professional class is the growing ranks of the so termed 'third sector' in the UK. NGOs and the voluntary sector agencies which are seeking more formal financial relationships to the state as paid for service providers.

4   For more of an indepth analysis of systems thinking see Chapman, J (2004) 'System Failure – why governments must learn to think differently'. Demos.

5   Research supported by Joseph Rowntree Foundation, and **nef**'s forthcoming people in public service.

A starting point

Elizabeth Cox

Change starts with the dream - only our imagination restricts us.

Over four years, we have proved that there is creativity in abundance, with the drive and personal passion to turn dreams into a business reality in 13 sufficiently diverse communities across England to be able to have our initial premise confirmed. *In every community, however economically disadvantaged, there are people who have a passion they could turn into a business.* We have had the opportunity to directly work with 1,400 at the time of writing, and this continues to grow.

We have also, over these past four years, reclaimed the term 'entrepreneur' from the ego-driven billionaire set – to be what it truly is: an attitude for enterprise, risk awareness and being ready to live the dream.

We have proved that enterprise can and should be at the heart of regeneration; that support of the individual's dream within a community, when it is being mobilised through local networks to share skills, knowledge and resources – because ultimately people care about their local area, their environment and their neighbours – can make business an exercise in collaboration, instead of ruthless competition. Business can become a place where social, economic and environmental impacts can be balanced.

The role of regeneration should be about finding ways to release the inherent energy in communities to claim back the power to reinvent themselves. This requires a complete re-thinking of the system. It means moving it from targets to values, and ultimately becoming a learning system – responsive, flexible and driven by the achievement of well-being for the citizens of planet earth.

Our challenge to ourselves is to remain true to our values going forward. We have a product, BizFizz, which has been a liberating experience to work on – and in going forward to share this with other agencies and communities, we have to maintain the integrity of the approach, whilst being open to new learning.

This means not becoming finance-driven junkies, chasing the next funding opportunity and screw the values in the meantime, but remaining true to our client focus, word-of-mouth promotion, belief in the people we work with, and our role of demonstrating a different way of working and a new system of support based within communities. It also means making sure we procure as many goods and services for the programme as we can from the communities we work with, and so putting our money where our mouth is to support local enterprise.

The driver for us in our work is challenging the current patterns of economic life that are destructive in terms of human and environmental poverty. Seeking out and demonstrating the alternatives to the status quo, that will deliver opportunities for people in communities and well-being, means we can change those values – and see the individual as a person, not as a number.

Our work continues. The glamorous appeal of the one-size-fits-all approach still persists. We have yet to meet the *universal entrepreneur* who matches the standard package offer, or the community – in the UK or internationally – that responds according to a policy blueprint for change. But we are beginning to see a shift in language in policy-makers and practitioners. Coaching is starting to appear in other programmes and agencies. In some cases we know this is a re-labelling process. However, it is still a recognition of the success of this way of working. Our next challenge will be to make this shift more than a mere cosmetic language change, and to influence a fundamental change in practice, values and attitudes.

We believe this approach provides a starting point for an alternative to the top-down initiatives in international development, where people are still counted as beneficiaries, and participation is about more people involved in supplying the consultants with data for them to make a decision.

What would the world look like if regeneration and development practice shifted to valuing dreams, harnessing energy and passion from within communities, delivering models built on trust? BizFizz shows it is possible and gives us a glimpse.

Change starts with the dream that something different is possible – you just have to take that leap of faith to go exploring.

Appendix 1
The BizFizz methodology in brief

1. **Community support**

   We insist that there is significant support within the community before we work with community leaders to initiate a BizFizz project. An approach that relies on harnessing the support of community members must have local support from the outset. If communities are to be truly put in the driving seat of transforming their local economies, they must be afforded the choice of whether they want the project in the first place. At the outset of a project, BizFizz visits each community and persons identifying themselves to form the initial local management group and panel, to establish if BizFizz feels it is relevant, and if it wants to be part of it.

2. **Community focus**

   BizFizz puts a coach at the heart of a relatively small geographic community. The coach gets to know local people, their aspirations, hobbies, interests and organisations, and becomes the focus for business support in that community. We recommend the size of the community is between 8,000 and 15,000 people. However, we have provided support up to 28,000 as, ever the pragmatists, we feel that putting artificial boundaries around areas is ridiculous. However, if you offer a fully flexibly service, you have to live up to this claim, and spreading the coach over a wider area can only mean they will have to ration their services.

3. **Entrepreneur focus**

   The coach's support is focused on helping individuals overcome barriers, whatever they may be, to pursue their business passion. The coaches do not operate strategically; they are 100 per cent client-focused in their support.

4. **Passion**

   The coaches work by identifying the passion of their clients to do something. The coach only works with clients who demonstrate passion for what they are doing, and encourages clients to follow their passion as the basis for a business idea. There is only one entrepreneur in the relationship and that is the client – the pace of that relationship is set by the client.

5. **Support networks**

BizFizz recognises that entrepreneurs do not normally have all the skills, or an interest, in all areas of the business. We address this by encouraging our clients to build up networks of support or temporary teams – for example to help with finance or marketing – through favours, sub-contracting, profit-sharing deals and bartering.

6. **Freedom**

BizFizz coaches are not restrained by the need to ration their service to their clients, nor do they adhere to notions of professional distance. They are free to do whatever is necessary, within reason, and without creating dependency, to remove the barriers to their clients' success. They are not bound to a desk, a desk-top computer or traditional working practices or hours. There is no rule book saying how a coach can and can not support their clients; they are professionals who provide tailored support to clients according to the client's agenda using their professional judgement.

7. **The panel**

BizFizz establishes a panel of 20–30 local people from a wide range of backgrounds. The panel meets monthly and considers 'cases' from the coach's clients. The cases consist of practical barriers to business success which the coach is seeking assistance from the panel to overcome. The panel attempts to find practical solutions using its:

- Contacts.

- Local knowledge.

- General knowledge and creativity.

www.bizfizz.org.uk

Appendix 2
Fitting in

Community support

By mobilising community support for a local BizFizz project, we make sure that:

- Word-of-mouth promotion encourages people, even those lacking confidence, to approach the coach for support.

- There is strong goodwill towards businesses established and supported through BizFizz.

- Local knowledge and networks can be tapped into to overcome barriers to success.

Community-focused

By putting the coach at the heart of the community we make sure that:

- The coaches can promote themselves directly through face-to-face meetings with local groups, individuals and businesses.

- The coaches are always available (within reason) and can be consulted without an appointment, increasing the likelihood that people lacking confidence will see them at the point when they are most motivated.

- The coaches can directly intervene to overcome local problems or make links locally.

Entrepreneur-focused

By putting the emphasis on supporting the entrepreneur, BizFizz makes sure that support is given where and how it is needed to overcome any practical or psychological barriers. The crucial role of the entrepreneur in driving the business is recognised.

Passion

The emphasis on passion as the driver of entrepreneurial behaviour means that we focus on what our clients actually want to do. Motivation is therefore much stronger and this helps to overcome lack of confidence and other more tangible barriers.

Support networks

By recognising that entrepreneurs cannot be good at, or enjoy, everything and that approaches such as training to fill skill gaps may not be appropriate, we make sure that new business people take a realistic view of themselves and their limitations and have a greater chance of success. The process of building support networks also builds social capital and cohesion in the community.

Freedom

The barriers preventing people in disadvantaged areas fulfilling their dreams come in many shapes and sizes. It is important for coaches to act as flexibly as possible to help entrepreneurs overcome them. The freedom given to coaches means they can do whatever is necessary to overcome barriers to success, whether that is spending four hours with one client, phoning an overseas supplier or knocking on the door of someone who might have space that could be used for business premises.

The panel

The panel helps people in disadvantaged communities overcome the barriers to business success by giving them a huge network of local knowledge and contacts that can be used to help their business. This means that those who were previously disadvantaged now have a huge advantage. By participating in the panel, significant sections of the community find ways to become more creative and entrepreneurial.

Appendix 3
The benefits

BizFizz brings a wide variety of benefits for communities and the people and organisations within them.

- Local entrepreneurs get support in the form they want it: friendly, flexible, non-judgemental, without trying to sell them training or some other form of programme. They create jobs and circulate wealth locally.

- Local businesses, both large and small find an excellent way to become engaged in regeneration. Business people normally resist sitting on committees, but the practical slant of the BizFizz panel is right up their street.

- The community becomes more self-confident and develops more of a can-do attitude.

- Mobilising people to help each other has a wider effect as people realise that a thriving local business community is in everyone's interests. Community projects and social enterprise ideas spin-off from the local panel networking.

- All sorts of other connections start to be made. In one pilot area, a local businessperson has decided to invest in creating some business units as a result of being on the BizFizz panel.

- The culture of local organisations changes. Regulatory bodies such as planning, environmental health or the Inland Revenue start to solve problems instead of creating them.

- Other business support agencies find the number of referrals they get and the take-up of their services from BizFizz areas increases. BizFizz works with the existing support agencies to provide the best support for clients.